Author's Note

I have known Abram and his brother, Hy, since I was a little boy growing up in Hrubieszow, Poland. For a few years in the 1920s, Abram's maternal grandfather, Mendel Sztych, was my father Lejb's business partner, exporting food grains to Germany and other European countries. However, as Abram is nine years older than I, except for an occasional greeting, we had little to do with one another.

I spent three years in the Nazi concentration camps during World War II and emigrated to the United States in October 1947. Visiting Israel for the first time in 1954, I reconnected with Abram, Hy, and their families. We talked a great deal about our individual experiences during World War II. Our friendship grew and we visited each other and went on several vacations together.

After I heard Abram's story, I felt it was important that it be told to a larger audience. Since Abram did not want to write his autobiography, I suggested that I would do it. Abram is modest to a fault and was reluctant at first, but I finally convinced him that it was important for him, for his family, and for history to have a record of what he had accomplished while fighting the Nazis and helping to establish the State of Israel.

When Abram came to visit my wife Susie and I in 1994, I recorded his life story on nineteen audio tapes. Using this material as well as many subsequent conversations with him, I wrote *Abram*.

I owe a debt of gratitude to Conor Cruise O'Brien who wrote the magnificent book, *The Siege*. It was very helpful in providing me with the background of the Zionist struggle to establish the State of Israel.

Even today, at the age of 84, Abram doesn't think he has accomplished anything exceptional. He says, "Many people would have done what I did."

I ask the reader to judge for himself.

ABRAM

Also by Henry Orenstein

I SHALL LIVE

British Army of the Rhine

T/Capt A. Silberstein. 246859

It has been brought to my notice that you have performed outstanding good service, and shown great devotion to duty, during the occupation of Germany.

I award you this certificate as a token of my appreciation, and I have given instructions that this shall be noted in your Record of Service.

B. L. Montgomery

Field Marshal

Date   7th July 46   Commander-in-Chief, British Army of the Rhine

Commendation from Field Marshal Montgomery
for Abram's service during World War II.

ABRAM

THE LIFE OF AN ISRAELI PATRIOT

BY

HENRY ORENSTEIN

BEAUFORT BOOKS
NEW YORK

First North American Edition

Library of Congress Cataloging-in-Publication Data

Orenstein, Henry, 1923–
Abram : the life of an Israeli patriot / by Henry Orenstein.
p.   cm.
ISBN 0-8253-0503-9 (alk. paper)
1. Silberstein, Abram. 1917– . 2. Great Britain. Army. Jewish
Brigade — Biography. 3. World War, 1939–1945 —
Participation, Jewish. 4. World War, 1939–1945 — Personal narratives,
Jewish. 5. Jews, Polish — Palestine — Biography. 6. Palestine —
Politics and government — 1917–1948. I. Title.
D810.J4.068   1999
940.54'04—dc21   98-40631
[B]   CIP

Published in the United States by Beaufort Books, New York
Distributed by Midpoint Trade Books

2 4 6 8 10 9 7 5 3 1

Printed in the United States of America

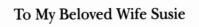

To My Beloved Wife Susie

CONTENTS

Illustrations after page 108.

ABRAM

~ 1 ~

GROWING UP
IN A LAND OF HATE

The shells were exploding all around. There was fear in Abram's heart, yet there was also a feeling of great excitement. "What is going on? Are the Bolsheviks shelling the Poles, or was it just the other way around?" In this crazy war, the opposing armies were moving back and forth, and it was difficult to tell who was occupying Hrubieszow at any given moment. Abram, like many boys involved in any war, any time, any place, was possessed by curiosity, by the desire to observe, to be part of the craziness, the brutality, the adventure that is war.

His father, Fishel, had no such feelings. In his mind, the safety of his family — survival — was the only thing that counted. He took Abram firmly by the hand and ran across the street to the cellar of his neighbor Benkel's big house, which he thought was safer. His instincts proved right. An artillery shell hit and destroyed most of the second story of the house where Fishel and his family lived.

Only a few days later, Abram, looked out from the window of his grandfather Mendel's house (which was about fifty feet from the house where Fishel lived) and watched with fascination as a group of about twenty Polish students set up a barricade on Lubelska Street. The boys, age about sixteen or so, were trying to help the Polish army under General Pilsudski beat off the assault of Soviet Bolsheviks on Poland. Alas, their ability to fight a real war didn't quite match their enthusiasm. From around the corner came about fifty Cossacks riding their small horses, waving their sabers, and screaming wildly. They overran the barricade. They cut the students literally to pieces, pursuing them as they tried to run for their lives. It was a horrible scene that remained embedded in Abram's mind forever. Boys, throwing themselves on the ground, running, crying, blood all over their faces and limbs; the Cossacks rampaging in a killing frenzy. It was over in minutes. The boys' bodies were lying on the street, on the sidewalks, blood everywhere. Not a single Cossack was hurt while the Poles hardly had a chance to use their rifles.

Soon after this incident, there was another scare. Thousands of Bolsheviks, with distinctly oriental features, rode through the town. The people were scared — maybe the soldiers would kill, rob, and rape. Apparently, though, they were in a great hurry to pursue their enemy, and there was a great collective sigh of relief when nothing bad happened.

On another occasion, Petlura's* Ukrainian soldier-followers came. They were known for their outrages against the Poles, and especially the Jews. They beat and robbed people, but soon were pushed back by the Polish soldiers, who though a little more disciplined, were not above doing the same to the Jews.

There was a period of a few weeks when the Bolsheviks occupied Hrubieszow, and because of the continuous movement of the battlefront back and forth, food supplies were virtually cut off. Many people, including Abram's family, were hungry.

---

*A Ukrainian leader who, with his followers, unsuccessfully tried to establish an Ukrainian state. Eastern Ukraine became part of the Soviet Union. Western Ukraine was absorbed by the newly created Polish state.

One day Abram was in his yard, and a Russian soldier came past. He looked at Abram's face, gave him a part of a loaf of bread, and said, "Hey kid, you look hungry; take it."

Abram's grandfather, Mendel, was considered to be one of the richest people in town. This, of course, was by itself a cardinal sin for the Communists. Apparently, some Jews, who were jealous of him, denounced him as a "capitalist" to the Communist officer in charge. Mendel became aware of the danger and went into hiding. A Russian soldier literally rode his horse into Mendel's living room looking for him. Abram's brother, Mojshe (Moniek), was sick in bed. The Russians caught a man they thought was Mendel, brought him into the house and prepared to shoot him. The women started crying and pleading that they had the wrong man. Finally they convinced the soldiers of their error, and thus saved the man's life.

Yes, these were dangerous and trying times and they had a strong, formative influence in shaping Abram's view of the world. Abram was born in Wyszkow, near Warsaw, on April 25, 1914. His grandfather, Noah Silberstein, lived with his wife, Rivka, and their children, David, Hersh-Binem, Rachel, and Abram's father, Efraim-Fishel, in Warsaw, although they moved for a few years to Wyszkow. At a time when most Jews were deeply religious, wore black kaftans, and went to synagogue at least once a week, Noah was different. He was one of the few who wanted to be a bourgeois European in dress and behavior. A leading and highly respected expert in forestry, he travelled all over Europe and Russian Siberia. He was a courageous man, an elegant dresser, and knew all about trees. Most of his business was done for his own account, but his advice was eagerly sought by tree growers and lumber merchants everywhere. This was in sharp contrast to Mendel Sztych, Fishel's father-in-law, who lived in a small town where emancipation had not reached most Jews; even though quite rich, he was much more traditional and religious. Perhaps this profound difference between Abram's two grandfathers' life-styles and religious outlooks is what caused a rift between them to the point where they never talked to each other.

Noah taught Fishel all he knew about the lumber business. Fishel developed close ties to a number of German lumber businessmen on his own. They learned they could trust him personally, as well as his business judgment. He had perfect command of the German language, travelled often to major German cities, and was making good money. Fishel met Tauba Sztych on one of his trips, and married her in 1909. They had three sons, Moniek born in 1911, Abram, and Chaim, who was born in 1917.

When lumber became scarce in the area, and Fishel had a tough time making a living, he switched to dealing in grain. He and his family moved to Hrubieszow in 1916 where his father-in-law, Mendel Sztych, was the most prominent grain dealer in the entire region, and who helped him get started in his new business.

The name of the town, Hrubieszow, originated from the old Polish word "rubieza" meaning frontier, as indeed it was on the Russian border. In the past the town probably served as a defensive outpost — the heart of the town was actually an island. The river, Huczwa, coming from the west, split into two branches before it reached the town, encircled it, and then the branches rejoined on the other side. The center part of the town was elevated, especially in the north, and the plains on the other side of the river were about 200 feet lower. In the spring, after the snow and ice had melted, the plains around the town were completely flooded. Later in the year, they provided excellent pastures for horses, cows, and flocks of white geese.

Abram's childhood house was right on the edge of the elevated ground, with an impressive view of the plains, ending again with the slightly elevated fields. Close to the house were several flights of wooden steps leading down to the lower section along the river. There stood a row of small wooden houses where the poor people lived in constant danger of spring floods. This section was called the "Wanes" and was inhabited by all kinds of tradesmen: rope makers, fishermen, carpenters, coachmen, porters, etc. Anyone living in the "Wanes" was marked indelibly as a person of lower class.

The heart of the town was formed by a big piazza surrounded on four sides by brick houses. The tallest, a three-story building, belonged to the well-known and wealthy Orenstein family. There were a few other well-to-do families, among them the Sztychs, the Regles, and the Brands. Their names meant status and wealth in a town of eight thousand Jews and seven thousand Poles.

Two gothic-style Catholic churches pierced the skyline. Just opposite the bigger church with the *gymnazjum* (secondary school) attached to it was a Russian Orthodox church with a number of onion-dome towers.

Hrubieszow had a large, impressive synagogue *(shul),* a two-story brick building with big, arched windows, completely out of proportion to the size of the town's population. Directly opposite the big shul there was a row of "sztiblech," small wooden, single-room buildings where "hasidim" belonging to different groups (who were sometimes very hostile to each other), did their praying and theological studies. There were the Radishizer, Belzer, or Kocker hasidim, each under the strict domination of their own Rebe.

There were two hospitals. The larger one was Polish; the smaller one Jewish. There was a Jewish Zionist primary school called Hatikva. The town had two small cinemas-theaters, and two separate cemeteries (for Jews and Gentiles).

Poles and Jews lived side by side for centuries, but never mixed. They spoke different languages, belonged to different religions, dressed differently, and represented altogether different cultures. It was obvious that the Jews did not belong there. They were out of place. Not being permitted to own land, the great majority lived in town. Many of the Jews were scholars. To all Jews education was of utmost importance, while Polish peasantry was, with small exceptions, illiterate.

Friction was constant and hatred prevalent, often intensified by Catholic priests. The younger Jewish generation understood that they were in an impossible situation. They did not, and could not, follow in the footsteps of their religious fathers because this led them nowhere. They broke away from religion and looked towards Communism, Bundism,* and Zionism. Their lives were in turmoil.

Noah, who had lost his wife many years earlier, was getting old. He became quite ill with asthma and moved to Hrubieszow. He was bedridden most of the time and had to be taken care of. Fishel, Tauba, and their three sons lived on the second floor of a house located on Mendel's property. (After their apartment was practically destroyed by an artillery shell, they moved to the first floor apartment.)

Fishel, with his father-in-law's help, also dealt in lumber and grain, but was never able to make a lot of money. His main interest was Zionism. He had a good knowledge of Hebrew and organized a circle of Hebrew speaking Zionists in Hrubieszow. He was an intelligent and talented man. Fishel loved music and played the fiddle very well. An excellent speaker, he was always the focus of every gathering, always with a joke fit for the occasion. He was one of the directors of the local Jewish school, Hatikva. He presided over the Jewish orphanage and the Jewish hospital, and was involved in the "Gmina" (the Jewish town council). In 1936 he became a member of the Directorate of the Keren Hayesod of Poland. In that capacity he worked closely with Dr. Moshe Kleinbaum (later known in Hebrew as Sneh). Together they travelled to almost every town in Poland

---

*Bundism: the bundists were fighting for Jewish rights and Jewish equality in Poland, where they wanted to remain.

until Sneh's departure for Palestine in 1937, where he was appointed by Ben-Gurion as head of the Haganah.

Abram's mother, Tauba, was one of the local beauties, and an excellent housekeeper. Her father, Mendel Sztych, was a very unusual man. He was born in Zamosc where he learned about the grain and lumber business from his father, Chaim. He wanted to be on his own, so after he married a local girl, Pesia, they moved to Hrubieszow. Mendel was very bright, hardworking, and soon the people in Hrubieszow developed a great deal of respect for his business savvy and integrity. He exported grain and lumber to Germany and other European countries. He loved horses, and there were always a few in his stable. Abram was his favorite grandson and Mendel saw in him the same love of nature, fields, forests, and animals that he himself had.

Abram was very different from other boys. He was handsome, tall for his age, wiry, with black hair and black penetrating eyes. Abram was a dreamer. He loved to tend to his grandfather's three horses, to feed and ride them. Alone, he walked through the fields and the woods. Abram started to observe and understand life around him. He was a boy of nature, and nature was his religion. Neither teaching nor preaching could ever influence his way of thinking. He hated the Orthodox Jews, the way they lived, dressed, and looked. He was very handy. If some work was in process in his grandfather's yard, he had an urge to observe it. He would stay with the workmen until the job was finished. His mother had a hard time getting him to come in for a meal. She knew she could always find him in the stable around the horses or with the workers.

Abram still recalls, as a six year old, the day when a team of Polish workmen put up a wooden gate in front of Mendel's house. He stayed with them watching them all day. It was already evening, but they couldn't finish the job because they ran out of big nails that they needed to join the planks. Abram asked them, "Why don't you drill a hole and put in a wooden pin?" The workers were astounded; the idea was perfect for the job. On completion of the work, the foreman took little Abram by the hand and asked to see his father. After a long search, they found him. With his hat off, the foreman said to Fishel, "Sir, this boy will be an excellent engineer. The advice he gave us was very helpful."

Abram had a friend who lived at the end of Lubelska Street. He was a Jewish blacksmith and walked with a limp. Abram helped him pump air into his forge and with other things. The blacksmith was proud as a peacock, shouting to the passersby, "You see, that's Mendel Sztych's grandson. He is helping me."

One day little Abram worked up the nerve and asked for permission to make a nail — a special nail for horseshoeing. The blacksmith laughed at the boy, but let him try. In no time, Abram, beating the anvil like a professional, made a perfect nail. The blacksmith didn't believe his eyes. He said to Abram, "Make another one." In minutes he made another, even better than the first. The blacksmith went crazy running around and shouting to people about the nail this boy made. From that day on, Abram was given the job of making nails.

Abram went to school at the age of eight. He did not like it. Even though he was a quick study, he didn't spend enough time on his homework to get good grades. His parents were unhappy about that, but that didn't bother Abram. He built his own kayak that was the envy of all other boys. Even though he went to the local Rabbi to study the Talmud three times a week, he wasn't very interested in learning Hebrew or Jewish history.

He soon became aware that something was wrong with being a Jewish boy in Hrubieszow. In the grammar school, Polish kids taunted the Jewish ones about being dirty and being killers of Christ. Abram wasn't even sure who Christ was, but he knew he must have been someone very important. There was graffiti on many walls and fences stating "Kill the Jews," "Jews to Palestine," "Jews Cheat," or "Buy from your own (gentiles)."

Polish teachers looked away when Polish kids would hit their Jewish schoolmates or throw stones at them. Abram was a fighter, which the Polish kids respected so they left him alone. He excelled in sports, built boats, which also helped his standing with the other kids. But the fact that he personally did better than the other boys didn't help the unease, the feeling of insecurity. Weeks before Pesach (Passover), he heard his parents worrying about the accusations made by Polish priests and anti-Semites that Jews were killing Polish children and using their blood to make matzos, the traditional Passover substitute for bread.

Jews lived in Hrubieszow for about 500 years. By hundreds of thousands they fled the persecutions and pogroms in Western Europe, in particular during the Crusades. They migrated to the Eastern European countries — Poland, Russia, Lithuania, Latvia, Hungary and others. These countries were mostly uncivilized and subject to repeated invasions from the East (Ghengis Khan and the Turks among others), but still they were a safe haven compared to Germany, France, and England.

The Jews were restricted by local ordinances from owning land, attending schools, obtaining higher education, and many other endeavors. So they became moneylenders, traders in grain, timber, and other commodities. They owned stores. They were tailors, shoemakers, candlemakers, and blacksmiths. They were very religious and clannish. They dressed differently and spoke Yiddish (a language which evolved by using mostly German and some Slavic words). Except for a relatively small number of emancipated families, they spoke a broken Polish, and amazingly, some of them didn't speak Polish at all.

Life was hard; many people did not have enough money to buy bread for their children who usually looked pale and had hollow cheeks. The Polish peasants were not much better off. They tilled the land owned by the big landowners, and lived by selling grain they were allowed to keep for themselves to the Jews. Poles who lived in towns were not much better off, with the exception of the clergy, town officials, and professionals like teachers, doctors, and lawyers. The Polish and Jewish communities had little contact with each other except for business at hand.

Given the circumstances, to many Jews life on this earth was secondary to the life in the hereafter, and they clung to their religion and traditions to make sure that nothing would endanger their standing with God. Most Poles resented the Jews. The priests told them every Sunday that Jews were not to be trusted, that they killed Christ, and were still killing Polish children. Jews were fearful of the pogroms and other abuses. Some who tried to assimilate into Polish society were laughed at and rejected. It was a no-win situation. If you tried to be like the Poles, they rejected you; if you didn't, they resented you for being different.

As Abram was growing up, the situation of Polish Jews kept deteriorating. The power of the Endeks (an organization of Poles whose prime agenda was to get rid of Jews) was growing. The boycott of Jewish stores became more intense. Even the Polish prime minister made headlines by saying, "Owszem" (It's okay.) It was okay with the government to put the Jews out of business, but not to actually kill them. The rising Polish merchant class fanned the flames of the anti-Jewish hatred. They couldn't compete with the Jews fair and square because Jews were smarter and more experienced, so they wanted to get rid of them one way or another.

Abram finished grammar school and was accepted to the gymnazjum (high school). Only a few Jewish children were allowed in, but Mendel had a lot of pull with the local officials and arranged it. The situation of the Jewish students there was even worse than in the grammar school. Most of the gymnazjum teachers were vicious anti-Semites. The Polish kids, having grown up in an atmosphere of hate, with Jews being constantly harassed and ridiculed, pushed the Jewish students around and taunted them.

Abram was not a good student in gymnazjum either. He was

not interested in studies, and did just enough homework to get passing grades. He spent most of his time building boats and painting. To his own surprise he found that he had a talent for painting. He was a proud boy and always stood up and was ready to fight when the Polish kids tried to intimidate him. Abram had a lot of inner strength, a strong feeling about what was right and what was wrong, and the courage to defend his rights.

There was a boy in Abram's class whose name was Wolff. His family came to Hrubieszow from Germany. His father was an engineer in the sugar factory of Szczyzow. Wolff was seated at a desk in front of Abram. He kept annoying Abram by leaning back, poking and pushing him. Abram knew that the teacher would take Wolff's side, even though he was the troublemaker. He tried to avoid a fight. One day, Abram was sharpening his pencil with a knife when Wolff suddenly turned around and hit him. Abram, by reflex, raised his arm to blunt the blow, and the knife went into Wolff's arm. This was real trouble. The teacher wanted Abram ejected from school. Mendel went to the head priest of the church in Hrubieszow who was very influential, and pleaded with him for help. He made a donation to the church, and saved the situation. The school ordered the boys to walk together to school. Wolff never bothered Abram again. There was a Polish boy in Abram's class, a hunchback with a long nose. Since many Jews had prominent noses, his one big fear in life was that he could be mistaken for a Jew. Just because of that, he hated Jews. He often would say, "You Jews are no good," or "You are all bad." Abram's reply was, "The truth is, you would like to look like me."

Another boy, Kornas, saw Abram eating a sandwich during recess and Kornas told him, "I don't like to watch you eating this sandwich because I can see that you enjoy it. But I don't mind at all when you Jews build houses, because sooner or later they will all belong to us." Kornas, in later years, became the head of the anti-Semitic Endek organization in Poland.

The teachers weren't any better. One day Wanczyk, the art "professor" saw Abram's paintings. Himself a man of little talent, he became jealous, an enemy. Yet in spite of his feelings, Wanczyk used Abram to do decorations for school theatrical productions and other occasions. Still, he would often say, "Art is not a Jewish vocation." This talent for arts helped Abram. In spite of poor grades, the teachers let him pass because he was the only student capable of making, almost by himself, all the stage sets and other items of art that the school needed.

Another teacher, Przywara, a professor of natural sciences, was also an out-spoken anti-Semite. Once, he and his class were outdoors when they spotted a wild goose. It was unable to fly, but resisted being caught with his long, sharp beak. Przywara ordered the boys to capture the goose. All, except for Abram, were afraid to do it. He stepped forward and quickly caught the goose. Przywara was upset because it was a Jewish boy who was willing to take a chance of being cut. He said, "I guess you should be selling geese in the market," and kept making other derogatory remarks about Jews.

There were exceptions. Abram's math professor, Swiedzinski, stood out among the others. He was a charming man, very sympathetic and understanding of the Jewish problems in all walks of life. Later during the war, he saved the life of a Jewish girl by hiding her in his house. He was a member of the Resistance. Someone betrayed him and he was shot and killed by the Germans.

Abram's older brother, Moniek, excelled in most subjects, especially in math. He was a sickly boy, frequently catching a cold or the flu. He studied at Warsaw University and supported himself by teaching math to other students in spite of his continuous heart problems. He was too proud to accept any help, expecially from his parents, knowing that they were going through hard times. Chaim, the youngest, was not interested in studying. He was exceptionally handsome, and was always followed by girls, both shiksas (gentile girls) and Jewish girls. Abram always protected Chaim from other boys who were jealous of his good looks.

Mendel continued to prosper. His business enabled him to fully support, or in some cases, help his family. His son, Josel, was a disappointment as a businessman. He thought his father didn't give him enough leeway and he left town, bitter against his family. Mendel took on a partner, Lejb Orenstein, and together they became by far the biggest dealers in grain in the entire area. Lejb had a reputation as a fighter, a risk taker, but some people in town gave the credit for Lejb's success to his wife, Golda. They thought she guided him and that she was the real brains of the family.

One day Moniek asked Abram to take a book over to the Orenstein house and give it to one of the Orenstein's sons, Shlomo. Golda apparently liked the boy and got into a conversation with him. She asked him how he was doing at school. Abram said he didn't care, he didn't study too much. Golda said, "That is no good. Leave the painting to the goyim (gentiles), study. Painting will not help you in life." Abram was very touched. No one ever talked to him as an adult. Golda was down to earth and logical and she made a great impression on him. She talked to him for almost an hour — he never forgot it. He liked her children. The youngest son, Henry, looked just like his mother, and was very respectful. The daughter, Hanka, was a pretty little girl. Shlomo studied law, and the two other sons, Fred and Felek, were in France studying medicine (very few Jews were accepted into the Polish universities).

Mendel died unexpectedly in 1928 after a bout with the flu, which was followed by a heart attack. This was a great shock to the Sztych and Silberstein families, in fact, to the entire town. Abram didn't know how to deal with it. How could it be that his beloved grandfather was suddenly no longer with them? It was as if someone suddenly removed a rock on which his entire life, his security, was based. For days he would walk around in a stupor, trying to absorb the reality of life, but it was hard.

Josel took over the management of the family business. However, he was a selfish man. He was so anxious to avoid distributing the money to his four sisters and two brothers, that he lent all the cash in the business to Polish land owners without regard for their poor credit or obtaining security. The result was, that in a couple of years, he lost it all. Lejb Orenstein did not want to continue to be partners with him, and Josel lost not just the money, but the respect of his family and the people in town. Because of him, Mendel's other children, including Abram's father, Fishel, were left in bad financial straits.

Josel, disillusioned and disgraced, emigrated to Palestine in 1933. His sister, Clara, divorced her husband and also went to Palestine, taking her son with her. Miriam, Mendel's youngest daughter, followed them with her husband and daughter. They were all helped by Abram's Uncle Mattes, who by that time had established a successful medical practice in Tel Aviv.

After Mendel's death things were not the same for the Silbersteins. Fishel struggled in the grain trade but couldn't quite make a go of it. He quit the business and became an official of the Keren Hajesod (the Jewish National Fund). This was an important and respected position, but the pay was poor. Abram's mother, Tauba, had to improvise to feed her family. They lived mostly on vegetables and bread. Only occasionally was she able to buy some eggs, and once in a while, chicken for the Sabbath dinner. In spite of the fact that they lived in real poverty, Fishel didn't have the heart to say no when someone else was hungry.

One day, just after he received his small salary from Keren Hajesod, Fishel was on the way home when he was approached by Bernstein, a man he knew who was out of work. Bernstein asked for help, and even though Fishel knew that the money he had with him meant food for his own family, he didn't have the heart to refuse him, and gave him almost all of it. In the meantime, Tauba was waiting for him and when Fishel came home and told her what had happened, she became furious. She asked, "And what about our own children?"

Abram felt lost. At school most of the Polish students and teachers were anti-Semitic. The streets were unsafe with Polish hooligans looking for any excuse to ridicule and sometimes physically attack Jews and their homes. He could see his parents struggling to keep the family going on very limited income. He had no idea what was going to happen to him and where he was headed. A new movie house was to be built in Hrubieszow, and a competition for the design for the front of the building was announced. A number of people competed for the prize money. Abram submitted his drawing and won. This gave his morale a needed boost, while providing the family with much needed extra money. Abram was spending most of his free time fishing, building boats, and reading. He liked to read books about the Wild West by the German author Karl May; Charles Dickens, and some of the Polish authors. But still he was bored, hyperactive, and had no patience to study. Lack of money caused some tension in the family. Abram could be stubborn, and sometimes Fishel, who was upset by the struggle to support his family, would slap him. Tauba always tried to protect Abram even when he was wrong.

Abram had friends like Appel and a few others, but he felt frustrated, with little confidence in his future. Even though many girls were pursuing him, he had no interest in them. He didn't relate to the religious Jews. He felt uneasy in their presence. Once he saw a Rabbi in white socks and a black kaftan walking on Lubelska Street towards the center of town. A whole bunch of Hassidic men with long payes (earlocks) were dancing around him as he was walking, vying for his attention. Abram, the artist, found this unesthetic. It somehow made everything Jewish look bad to him. He knew Poland was not his country — not his home. Yet he didn't identify strongly with

Jews either. He knew that as Poland was becoming more and more anti-Semitic, the outlook for his future there was bleak.

There were Jewish organizations like Zabotinsky's Betar, which was supported by nationalists, and Hashomer Hazair, which was socialistic. Many Jewish boys, knowing that there was no future for them in Poland, were joining them hoping that one day they would be able to emigrate to Palestine, even though the British were severely restricting immigration.

Abram didn't want to go to Palestine. He was confused. He graduated from the gymnazjum and received his diploma, but he knew that his father didn't have the money to send him to a university. He said to Fishel, "Let me go to France. I will study there and support myself." In his mind, France represented real civilization, a place where culture and art were admired. He felt that, perhaps, this was where he belonged. Fishel didn't want to hear about it. He told Abram, "I want you to go to Palestine."

In the meantime, Fishel's older brother, David and his wife, Rose, who lived in Warsaw, were about to emigrate to Palestine. This was done with the help of their eldest daughter, Sarah, a member of the Hashomer Hazair, who obtained the necessary documents. The kibbutz they went to live in was near Hadera whose members, despite not having any previous experience, were learning to cultivate the land which had been laying barren and untilled for 1,000 years.

While working for Keren Hajesod and seeing what was happening in Poland, Fishel became convinced that the best place for Abram's future was Palestine. Even though the British promised to establish a Jewish homeland in Palestine, they were dragging their feet, and it wasn't clear whether, faced with strong opposition from the Arabs, they would do so. Still Fishel felt that Palestine held the best prospects for Abram's future. Abram had no desire to emigrate to Palestine. The idea of Zionism was not appealing to him. But, he had great respect for his father and would not go against his wishes. About a month after his graduation, in June 1934, Fishel bought Abram a ticket that would take him to the Holy Land.

Abram travelled through Romania and boarded a boat in Constanza, on the Black Sea, and sailed to Haifa. From Haifa he travelled by bus to Tel Aviv.

~ 2 ~

A NEW LIFE IN PALESTINE

Jews, according to their calendar, arrived in the area that is Israel today about 3,500 years ago (ca. 1500 B.C.). Abraham and his tribe lived in the town of Harran in the northern Mesopotamian kingdom of Mitami. Historians claim that he was the first man known to believe that there was only one God, which was quite a departure from the then prevailing religions which were based on believing in, and praying and making sacrifices to many gods (gods of war, harvest, good health, weather, love, and many others).

The reason for Abraham's leaving Mesopotamia is unknown; one could theorize that his religious beliefs caused trouble for him with neighboring tribes. For many centuries thereafter, his descendants grew in numbers, were ruled by many kings, and waged many wars — which sometimes resulted in mass expulsions of many of them to Egypt and the various kingdoms of Mesopotamia. These two areas were the power centers of the entire region, and the Jews who lived in between them were often caught in the middle of their wars. Their cities were destroyed and their citizens taken as slaves.

The Jews' capital, religious as well as political, was Jerusalem, which grew to be one of the largest cities in the Middle East.

When Rome became for many centuries the dominant power of the Mediterranean, Western Europe and the Middle Eastern regions, its legions enforced Roman law on its subjects. From time to time rebellions took place in Germany, France, North Africa, and the Middle East against the Roman Empire. Sometimes the rebel armies won individual battles, but in the long run, the disciplined and superbly trained Roman legions were always victorious. Jews revolted against the Romans under the leadership of Bar Kochba and were subdued by Trajan (115–117 B.C.) and Hadrian (132–135 B.C.).

In 63 B.C. the Roman General, and later Consul, Pompey, conquered the entire Middle East and largely destroyed the Jerusalem Temple and many others. The Jewish King, Herod, rebuilt it, lavishing great sums of money on construction. The Roman Procurators of Judea were very anti-Jewish and indifferent to Jewish religious sensibilities. Jews resented the high taxes they were forced to pay. All this brought on a bloody war with Rome in 66–70 A.D. The war ended with the destruction of Jerusalem and the second Temple again. The Roman general (and later Emperor), Titus, sought to spare them (according to Josephus, a Jewish traitor who joined the Roman army), but the Jews, especially the zealots, who were very nationalistic, refused to give in. They fought on until the end.

The Jewish population of Jerusalem during the siege grew to almost 2,000,000, as many of the inhabitants of towns and villages around it sought shelter from the advancing Roman legions. Hundreds of thousands of Jews were killed by the victorious Romans. Some escaped but hundreds of thousands more Jewish men, women, and children were taken as slaves and sent to Mesopotamia, to Egypt, to Rome, and many other places. Some of the escapees formed small groups of resistance. The best known of those put up a heroic stand on the

Masada Hill, where when they saw the end was near, they all committed suicide rather than face slavery.

This is how the Jewish Diaspora began, and it lasted for almost two millennia. From Egypt the Jews spread to other North African countries, and from there to Spain, Italy, Germany, France, and England. From Babylonia they went to the area of the Caucasusian mountains. There were periods when the Jews fared relatively well, particularly in North Africa's Muslim countries and in Spain, prior to the Inquisition which began in 1492.

During the Spanish Inquisition thousands of Jews chose to die at the stake rather than convert to Christianity. The Inquisition was responsible for a new wave of exiles to flee Spain for other western European countries and Turkey. The Christian Crusaders in the 11th to 13th centuries A.D. caused the flight of Jews from Western to Eastern Europe — the majority of them to Poland. The Crusaders were a motley army of adventurers, fanatics, and lower-class riffraff. Before departing for the Holy Land, they engaged in pogroms in the Jewish ghettos where they robbed, beat, and killed innocent Jews. After Catherine the Great, the Russian Tzarina, in partnership with Germany and Austria-Hungary dismembered Poland, Russia occupied Eastern Poland and the Ukraine, which at the time was part of Poland. Jews who lived in large numbers in these areas became Russian subjects. Many migrated to other Russian cities like Moscow and Petrograd. After the Crusades, Jews in Europe were no longer subject to large scale violence, but there were still restrictions on how they could earn a living, and obtain higher education. They lived in a continuous state of insecurity and fear of the authorities, as well as of their neighbors.

Over the centuries, Jews became hardened and ingenious in finding new ways to survive. They depended on their religion for moral support to withstand the hostility and jealousy surrounding them. They refused to change their ways, their clothing, or their habits in the face of hatred, scorn, and abuse. They clung to their religious leaders whom they respected more than anyone else. Century after century they dreamed of returning to Jerusalem. So strong were their bonds with their past that, instead of bidding each other a conventional "good-by," they would say, "Leshona haba B'Yerushalyim" (Next year in Jerusalem).

During the Diaspora, two different branches of Jews developed. Those who lived in North Africa and Spain were known as Sefardim. They fared better economically and suffered less persecution than their counterparts in Europe known as the Ashkenazim. The Sefardim produced many scholars, doctors, and philosophers, of which the best known is Maimonides, whose code of the Jewish law, Mishne Torah, remains to this day the only comprehensive treatment of all Jewish law. For the Ashkenazim life was more difficult, full of pogroms, oppression, and poverty, and only in the mid- and late-eighteenth century, were they able to engage in studies of philosophy and sciences in a significant way.

Moses Mendelsohn was, perhaps, the most outstanding Jew of his time. At first he was Orthodox, but turned away from the traditional Jewish preoccupation with the Talmud to become the foremost Jewish representative in the intellectual world of the European enlightenment. Mathematics, history, and literature were more important to him and his followers than traditional Jewish studies.

Napoleon was far more sympathetic to Jews than most of his contemporaries. He convoked a Sanhedrin (Jewish legislative council) in 1807 to create a modern definition of Judaism. All this led to some improvement of Jewish life in Western Europe in the early- and mid-nineteenth century. Even though the populace was still very anti-Semitic, some of the Christian western philosophers and intelligentsia became more sympathetic to the Jews. Schools of higher learning began accepting a number of them and thousands of Jewish boys (and a few girls) became doctors, teachers, lawyers, and scientists.

This emancipation continued without any major problems until about 1870. Then a new anti-Semitic wave hit Western Europe, particularly in Germany and France. Virulent anti-Semitic propaganda by Von Shoener, Neitzche, Lueger, Voltaire, Drumont and others accused Jews of corruption, treason (as shown in the infamous trial and conviction of Dreyfuss — engineered by the French army's top officers), and just about every bad trait one can find in a human being.

In Eastern Europe, dominated by the Russian Empire, Jews never had much of a chance. There were five million of them in Russia alone, most of them in the Pale and the Polish part of Russia. This was by far the greatest concentration of Jews in the world. After the assassination of Tsar Alexander II in 1881, pogroms were encouraged by his successor, Alexander III. Government officials were fanning the anti-Jewish sentiments of the populace. In 1881 a wave of 200 pogroms hit Jewish quarters in many towns and villages. This caused a massive emigration to the U.S., which at the time had an open door policy. A few joined the Russian revolutionary movement hoping to overthrow the Tsar. Others, seeing no future in Russia, dreamt of going to Palestine which was then occupied by the Turks in hopes of building and establishing a Jewish State.

Theodor Herzl (1860–1904), a Hungarian Jew, came to the conclusion that there was no future for the Jewish people in Europe; that there was no chance for them to be ever treated as equals. The first Dreyfuss trial convinced Herzl that Zionism was the only solution to Jewish problems. He published *Judenstaat* (*A Jewish State*) in 1889. Herzl was exceptionally tall, handsome, extremely intelligent, and full of life. He had great charisma; he was a showman. With his personality and presence, he gained access to the most powerful leaders of Europe — people who were beyond the reach of ordinary citizens. He was an unusual man. A man born, perhaps, once in a generation. He was successful in arranging meetings with the Pope; the German Kaiser, Wilhelm II; the Turkish Sultan, Abdul Hamid, and many other prominent Europeans.

Herzl arranged a congress of Zionist leaders from all over Europe that took place in Basel, Switzerland, in 1897. In a moving speech, Max Nordau said, "He (the Jew) lost his house in the ghetto. His countrymen repel him when he wishes to associate with them. He has no ground under his feet. He feels the world hates him, and he sees no place where he can find warmth." Chaim Weizmann (born in Pinsk, Russia, 1874–1952) attended the Second Zionist Congress in Basel in 1898. A world renowned chemist, he later became Herzl's successor in the leadership of the Zionist movement. The rich Jewish families of Western Europe also became uneasy with the new wave of anti-Semitism and began funding the Zionist movement.

At the same time the quality of Jewish life in Russia continued to deteriorate. Even those Jews who initially believed that they could be assimilated into the Russian population now knew that it was a lost cause. One of those, Leon Pinsker (born in Odessa, 1821–1891), published in 1882 *Auto-emancipation,* in which he wrote that in order to survive Jews must establish their own state. He and other Jewish leaders like him were responsible for convincing many young Russian Jews to emigrate to Palestine.

A new wave of pogroms came, and even the few remaining doubters lost all hope. In Kishinev, the capital of Bessarabia, on April 19 and 20, 1903, thirty-two men, six women, and three children were killed; five hundred were injured (of those eight more died of their wounds). One hundred women were raped; 1,500 Jewish homes were looted and destroyed. It was mostly the poor and uneducated Russians who did the damage, but they were encouraged by the upper class Russians.

So it was largely the anti-Semitism in Western Europe that opened the flow of money (particularly from Edmond Rothschild, a member of the famous banking family) needed to fund Jewish settlements in Palestine. The pogroms in Russia caused young Russian Jews to emigrate to Palestine and establish these settlements which were primarily agricultural. The combination of the Rothschild money, the efforts of Herzl and other Zionist leaders, and the enthusiasm and dedication of the Zionist Russian-Jewish boys and girls were responsible for the laying of the foundation for the future Jewish State, Israel.

Abram arrived in Palestine in the summer of 1934. Upon his arrival in Tel Aviv, he went to his Uncle Mattes' house and was warmly received by his relatives. As a young boy in Hrubieszow, Mattes was considered to be the "black sheep" of the family. He was very strong willed, and always did what he wanted to do. While in school in Kowel he had an anti-Semitic teacher. Because of him, Mattes decided that he had no future in Poland. In 1916 at the age of 13, he ran away from home and joined a Zionist group in Warsaw which was organizing the emigration of young Jews to Palestine. Without telling his parents — and without any papers or money — he joined a group of young Jews on their way to the Holy Land via Constantinople. The man in charge of the group liked Mattes and helped to smuggle him into Turkish occupied Palestine. Mattes was accepted to the Hebrew gymnazjum in Herzlia. Service in the Turkish Army was compulsory, and when his turn came, he ran away to Vienna to study medicine. After he received his degree, he returned to Palestine, opened his practice in Tel Aviv, and became known there as a brilliant doctor.

He was a very intelligent and generous man. He helped his family in many ways. He welcomed Abram with open arms and invited him to stay in his house. It so happened that the very same day the Finkelstein family arrived in Tel Aviv. They were Abram's Grandmother Pesia's friends, and they too were invited to stay in the Mattes' house. Abram could see that it was getting crowded, so he left and walked to the Mediterranean seashore where he spent the night sleeping on the sand. It was summer, it was warm, and he slept well. He was enchanted by the sea, by the waves gently rolling onto the shore. At sunrise, birds were flying over his head and making a lot of noise while hunting for fish.

Abram felt good. There was freedom in the air. He felt at home. He went to Mattes' house, had breakfast, and started walking around Tel Aviv. Late in the day he ran across Greenberg, a man he knew in Hrubieszow, and who, upon learning about the crowd at the Mattes' house, invited Abram to stay in his small apartment. As Abram walked the streets of Tel Aviv he saw a lot of construction going on. All the workers were Jews. Tel Aviv was then a small town growing fast, hustling and bustling with crowds of mostly very young Jewish boys and girls. The Arabs lived in the old city of Jaffa, to the south of Tel Aviv.

Abram was able to get a job with a construction company. He rented a small room in town, and for the first time in his life he felt really happy. He was making 35 grosz a day (one British pound was worth 100 grosz), which was enough to cover his basic needs. In the evening he was working for an architect, which helped him acquire knowledge of some technical vocabulary. When he started earning more money and had steady employment, he applied to the British authorities for a certificate that would allow his parents to join him in Palestine.

To his dismay, he received a reply which was both brief and negative. The reason for the rejection seemed ridiculous. His parents were too young to be supported. The British were turning increasingly negative toward Jewish immigration, perhaps because they didn't want to antagonize the Arabs.

Then a terrible tragedy befell the Silberstein family. Their beloved brother, Moniek, died at the age of twenty-five of heart failure. He died on a train that was taking him to a hospital in Aleksandrow, near Warsaw. He was buried in the Aleksandrow Jewish cemetery. Abram's parents kept the death a secret from Abram for two months.

There was a tremendous enthusiasm among the young Jewish pioneers in Palestine. During the day they were busy building, working at their jobs. In the evening and late into the night, they were in the streets, happy, talking, singing, and dancing. Life was hard, but there was an enormous feeling of camaraderie, of freedom, of joy, of common purpose. Abram felt as if someone lifted a huge stone from his shoulders — a weight he had carried since he was a child. For the first time in their lives, he and the other immigrants tasted real freedom; freedom from oppression, freedom from fear. They were building their own country. They believed in their future, even though they knew many obstacles lay ahead. The feeling of belonging, of a common cause was overwhelming, but they enjoyed every minute of it. At the time, the tension between the Jews and the Arabs was at a low level, and the British, who under their mandate ruled Palestine, were not really hostile to the Jews. All this, though, was a temporary lull before the storm.

Chaim Weizmann, who at the time was assuming the moral leadership of the Zionist movement, was selling the idea of a Jewish entity-state to his friend, Arthur Balfour, in 1914, even before Word War I began. In 1916, a new British Tory government came into power, headed by David Lloyd George. Balfour became the Foreign Secretary. Turkey, which occupied Palestine for hundreds of years, elected to join Germany and Austria-Hungary in the war, fighting against Great Britain, France, Russia, and later the United States.

The British wanted Palestine for strategic reasons; it would provide added security for their Suez Canal and a passage to India, the jewel of their worldwide empire. The new Tory government supported Zionism in order to gain the sympathy of American and Russian Jews who they believed could be helpful in enlisting their respective governments in the war against the Central European powers.

It is interesting to note that the German government had

similar ideas of how important the American Jews were, and in order to gain their sympathy, they convinced the Turks to remove restrictions on Jewish emigration to Palestine.

Abram continued to work at construction and each day felt more confident about his own abilities and the future of Jews in Palestine. Most buildings in Tel Aviv were two or three stories high, and there were many small stores and restaurants. There was a good feeling among the young people. They were building something for themselves — if not a country, at least a home. There were many kibbutzim in Palestine, and the kibbutzniks frequently visited Tel Aviv to buy supplies and see relatives. Abram's cousin Sara lived with her father David in a kibbutz. During one of Abram's visits David complained that there was no shade over the open veranda where he liked to sit. Abram constructed a small, screened roof for him. Suddenly a committee of kibbutzniks appeared and created a fuss over what they considered to be a special luxury for one individual. They wouldn't tolerate individualism. Abram decided that kibbutz was not his kind of life; he didn't want anyone to tell him how to live.

The kibbutzim played a critically important part in the life of Jewish immigrants. They learned — and they taught other Jews — the skills of farming, of building, of being independent and proud. But the structure of a kibbutz was very much along Marxist lines. You contributed as much as you were able to, but you received only according to your needs. One had to be very idealistic to accept this kind of life, but thousands of these young people were happy to have freedom from oppression, to be building something for themselves, and they were willing to make the personal sacrifice.

Most of the kibbutzniks were young, and even though they grew up in the religious atmosphere of the European shtetl, once they arrived in Palestine many rejected the moral code of their parents and their forefathers. Some "lived" with their girlfriends without giving much thought to marriage. Changing partners was no big deal. It was a completely new breed of a Jew — cosmopolitan, enthusiastic, exuberant, idealistic, hard working and loving it.

Young Jews living in towns were also excited about their new lives, but to them sharing of their lives and belongings, as was the case in the kibbutz, was not appealing. Abram would not even contemplate the kibbutz lifestyle. Even as a boy in Poland he would stand up and fight for his rights and for his pride, although this often meant fights with anti-Semitic Polish kids.

❧ 3 ❧

THE JEWS, THE ARABS,
AND THE ENGLISH

The future of the Jewish immigrants, in spite of all their enthusiasm, had many clouds on its horizon. The relations among the British, Jews, and Arabs was, to say the least, complicated and full of conflicting interests. On December 11, 1917, British field Marshall Edmund Allenby took Jerusalem from the Turks, thus ending centuries of Turkish rule in the Holy Land. He entered the old city on foot through the Jaffa gate followed by his victorious soldiers. In December 1918, the population of Palestine consisted of 512,000 Muslims, 62,000 Jews, and 61,000 Christians. As a result of their victories in World War I, the British took over the control of Iraq and Palestine. They wanted to secure the Middle East as a bridge to the "jewel" of the Empire — India. Most of them felt that the Balfour Declaration of November 2, 1917, which called for the establishment of a Jewish Homeland (not necessarily a state) in Palestine, was not in Britain's best interests, and they didn't permit its publication of it in the Middle East. The Arab nationalists, especially toward the end of World War I, sensed that the collapse of the Ottoman Empire might give them an opportunity to establish their own state in Palestine. They could see that the growing number of Jews, now backed by the Balfour Declaration, would create a difficult obstacle in fulfilling their dreams.

Sir Ronald Stokes was appointed Governor of Jerusalem in 1917 and ruled until 1925. He was not anti-Jewish, as some had charged but he wasn't interested in changing anything either. He was artistically inclined and paintings and sculptures were of more interest to him than Jewish or Arab ambitions. The British military establishment, however, became even more anti-Zionist with the Balfour Declaration and did their best to reverse it.

From 1919 on, Arab nationalism was on the rise. Their leaders, like Rashid Rida and Shurki El Assali, were warning their countrymen of the Jewish danger. They were worried about the Zionists, and knew that Arabs were not able to compete with Jewish merchants and craftsmen. Between April 4th and 8th Arab rioters attacked the Jewish quarters of the Old City of Jerusalem. Five Jews were killed and more than 200 injured. The British Army stood by and, even worse, it forbade the Jews to organize their own defense. Zabotinsky tried to do it and was arrested. There were some negative reaction in Britain and, as a result of the pogrom, the military administration was replaced by a civilian one headed by Sir Herbert Samuels, an English Jew and Zionist sympathizer. The Colonial Office issued in 1922 what became known as the *White Paper*. It stated that the establishment of a Jewish National Home should be internationally recognized and rested its case on the ancient historical Jewish background in Palestine. At the same time it reassured the Arabs that a Jewish National Home didn't mean a Jewish State. From 1922 until the outbreak of World War II in September 1939, British policy was to allow to some limited extent the building of a Jewish National Home. The British attitude was one of masculation, reflected in the ups and downs of the number of Jewish immigrants allowed to enter the British Protectorate. However, an important event occurred when Sir Herbert Samuels allowed the Jews to buy land by issuing a Land

Transference Ordinance. This Ordinance opened the doors to legal Jewish immigration to Palestine.

Winston Churchill, who at the time was the head of the powerful British Colonial Office, was also sympathetic to the idea of Zionism. He convened a conference in Cairo in March 1921 where he reached an understanding with Arab nationalist leaders. Faisal, the son of Shariff Hussein, was to be King of Iraq; and Abdullah, the other son, to be the Emir of Transjordan. From Cairo, Churchill went to Jerusalem. Jews welcomed him with open arms, but the Arabs were suspicious and didn't greet him with much enthusiasm.

By April 1921, 10,000 new Jewish immigrants had come to Palestine. They were young, highly committed Zionists who received prior training in farming in order to be prepared for a new life, particularly in the kibbutzim. At that time, the Arabs held an election to choose their Grand Mufti. Haj Amin al Hus-seini from Jerusalem, the instigator of previous anti-Jewish riots, came in fourth. He claimed fraud and used the occasion to organize new riots. On May 1, twenty-seven Jews and three Arabs were killed in Jaffa. In the days that followed, the riots spread and a total of forty-seven Jews and forty-eight Arabs were killed. Sir Herbert Samuels, in order to calm down the Arabs, appointed Haj Amin as Grand Mufti. A period of calm followed and from mid-1921 until 1929, there were no major incidents of violence in Palestine.

By 1922 the Jewish population in Palestine had grown to 84,000 and many of the British political and military leaders became worried about antagonizing the Arab population. The British started to push the idea of creating a Legislative Council in which Arabs would have a decisive majority. The Jews reluctantly agreed to participate in the Council, but the Arabs stupidly fought it because they didn't want any agency that would include even in a small minority Jews. The Jews began to realize that the British leadership — at best divided about the growing Jewish-Arab conflict — could not be relied upon for their security. As early as 1920 Jewish unease led to the establishment of the Haganah.* In the beginning there were only a few hundred part-time members. The Histadrut represented the trade unions.

Haj Amin became the most powerful Arab leader both in the religious and political arenas. He enjoyed strong support from the British, who believed that having more power would make him more responsible. Indeed, that seemed to be the case during the first few years of his rule as the Grand Mufti. The Jewish and the Arab communities enjoyed a great deal of autonomy, only loosely supervised by the British. Under the auspices of the Balfour Declaration the Jewish immigration to Palestine continued and reached 33,000 in 1925. Arthur Balfour himself visited Palestine in 1925 at the age of 77 to officially open Hebrew University where he was, of course, warmly greeted by the Jews. There were protests in the Arab press against him and his visit, but fortunately there was no new violence.

Restriction on American immigration, which came in 1924, was the main cause of the influx of Jews to Israel in 1925. Many European Jews who decided there wasn't much of a future for them in Europe, and whose first choice was America, chose their second best option and came to live in Palestine.

Sir Herbert Samuels retired in June 1925, and Baron Plumer was named his successor as Britain's High Commissioner for Palestine. He remained in that position until 1928. Plumer was a celebrated commander in World War I and was successful in his new post as well. He promoted the status quo in Palestine that included the idea of establishing a Jewish National Home as envisioned in the Balfour Declaration and the Mandate.

Vladimir Zabotinsky, a Polish Jew, became a hero to many Palestinian Jews owing to his leadership in the defense of Jeru-

*a paramilitary defensive Jewish organization

salem Jews during the riots of April 1920, and his subsequent jailing by the British. He was a hardliner as far as the relationship with the Arabs was concerned and was convinced that only a strong, armed Jewish population would be able to deal with the Arab threat.

The retirement of [now] Lord Plumer in July 1929, brought an end to the relatively quiet years in Palestine. Sir John Chancellor succeeded him, and the Grand Mufti, Haj Amin, began to sense that the British government was now leaning more towards the Arab side. He again started an incendiary anti-Jewish propaganda and organized demonstrations at the Wall (the only remaining wall of the ancient Jerusalem Temple) where he told the Arabs that their own holy places were now threatened by Jews. A series of local brawls led to violence in a number of towns. The British, who had reduced their police force, were unable to stop it. In August 1925, 133 Jews were killed and hundreds injured. A massacre of Jews took place in the city of Hebron, which had a small Jewish population. Six Arabs were killed.

Zabotinsky's idea of a Jewish "Iron Wall" had become popular among Jews and gained credibility even among his critics. This included David Ben-Gurion who was, until then, unalterably opposed to Zabotinsky whom he considered almost a Fascist. The killings of August made clear to the Jews that obtaining arms and training their young men and women was critically important to the survival of the Jewish community.

Haganah was now claiming that even their limited forces saved Jewish lives in major cities. Some of their more militant members began joining Zabotinsky's Betar, and from there, formed Irgun, an underground organization that promoted the policy of fighting terror with terror. As the feeling of insecurity increased, the Betar-Irgun coalition began gaining popularity. The events of August greatly increased the prestige and popularity of Haj Amin among his countrymen, and in fact, among the Arabs all over the world. He and his followers now believed that Jews were weak, and that they would be able to defeat them once the British left Palestine.

The First Royal Commission investigated the events, decided that the attacks on Jews were not premeditated and refused to fully blame the Mufti for them. They concluded that in order to prevent additional violence, the Jewish immigration should be more restricted. Sir Hope Simpson headed the Second Royal Commission and recommended, in the interest of peace, that a limit of 50,000 new immigrants a year should be put on Jewish immigration. This, in effect, would deal a death blow to the idea of the establishment of the Jewish National Home in Palestine.

More bad news was coming. Lord Passfield, a key member of the British government, used the reports of the Second Royal Commission to issue a new White Paper on October 21, 1930. He claimed that the British had fulfilled all their obligations to establish a Jewish National Home in Palestine as proclaimed in the Balfour Declaration of 1917. It became clear that Passfield's aim was to establish an independent Arab Palestine State with some protection for the Jewish population already there. Chaim Weitzmann became so upset with the idea of an Arab Palestine that he resigned as Chairman of the Zionist Organization on the very day the White Paper was published. Lloyd George, Samuels and Armory led the attack on the new White Paper in the British Parliament. Prime Minister McDonald at first defended it and then realized that it was a political mistake to do so. He was forced by the chain of events to read, on February 13, 1931, a letter to Weitzmann, in which he stated that a letter of clarification of the White Paper would be issued, and that it would become the "authoritative interpretation" of it. He told the House of Lords that Jewish immigration to Palestine and tenants on the land there would continue to be the obligation of the Mandate (without prejudicing the rights of others). The Weitzmann letter was immediately branded as the "Black Letter" by the Arabs. The entire affair turned out to be a great victory for Zionism.

Abram continued his work in the construction of commercial buildings, stores, offices, mostly in Tel Aviv, which was growing by leaps and bounds. He was getting better and better in his trade, and finally he became a foreman. Abram was very creative in his work, and his superiors were appreciative of his ideas of how to do things better and simpler. He became totally committed to the idea of building a new country. He was happy and so absorbed in everything that was going on that he had no time for girls, even though many of them approached this young, tall, good-looking man. Eventually Abram became a real expert in construction. He formed his own small group with some of his co-workers; he was the leader of this unit and obtained contracts from construction firms for complete projects.

Haganah was looking to expand their membership but they were interested only in very dedicated people who could keep their activities secret as they were still an illegal organization. They sought strong young men and women who had been in Israel at least a year and who would be willing to risk their lives for their cause. A man who worked with Abram approached him and said, "We need men like you."

Abram was asked to come to an initiation ceremony which was held at night in a big cellar of a local high school. There was a Haganah commission waiting for him. One of the commission members put a light in Abram's face and made him swear an oath of allegiance and secrecy. Secret training sessions followed in which members were taught the use of guns, grenades, and other weapons. He was given assignments consisting mostly of guarding Jewish homes and businesses in Jaffa, which at the time was predominately Arab.

Jaffa was occasionally patrolled by British military, and one night they caught him on duty carrying a gun. He was taken to a British military building, but was held there for only three hours. At the time Haganah had connections with the British police and they paid money for his release.

Hitler came to power in Germany in 1933, an event that had an enormous impact on the development of the Zionist society in Palestine and on the eventual birth of Israel, the first Jewish State in more than 2,000 years. During the 1933–1939 period, Nazi Germany actually encouraged Jewish emigration. Until Hitler came to power, German Jews were relatively well-off. They were given the opportunity to become lawyers, doctors, scientists, businessmen, and artists and were making important contributions to German society. They were very conscious of the persecutions, ghettos, and the lack of acceptance that existed for many centuries in Germany, France, England, and most other European countries and were extremely grateful for the chance they now had for a better life. Their appreciation was expressed by becoming more patriotic than many Christian Germans. They had an outstanding record of military service in the German Army in World War I with a rate of battle casualties and decorations higher than that of the average German. Now they found it difficult to accept and understand Hitler's anti-Semitic policies. They were bewildered by the Nazis' brutal attacks on them, by confiscations of their businesses and properties, by being denied the pursuit of their careers in Germany. Hoping that somehow the old order would be restored, they considered Hitler an aberration. As year after year went by, they could only see a worsening of their position. More and more of them began to accept reality and started to look for ways to get out. Although the Nazis made them pay a heavy financial price for the right to emigrate, tens of thousands elected this route.

The restrictive U.S. immigration policy in the 1930s made Palestine a good second choice, and the number of new immigrants rose from 4,000 in 1931 to 62,000 in 1935. By 1937 the Jewish population of Palestine reached 400,000. Almost fifty

percent of the newcomers came from Germany and it neighbors affected by Hitler's policies. The British policy was still restrictive and selective by accepting, almost exclusively, people
with a certain minimum of capital.

Hitler's rise to power in Germany and the dangers that
came with it convinced more and more Jews everywhere, but
particularly in Europe, of the necessity to create a Jewish State.
Jewish leaders, perhaps because of Hitler's threat, warned the
world of the impending disaster. Ben-Gurion who was issuing
warning after warning about Hitler's intentions, had an even
more detailed vision of events to come than Winston Churchill.
Said Ben-Gurion in January 1935:

> The disaster which has befallen German Jewry is not
> limited to Germany alone. Hitler's regime places
> the entire Jewish people in danger, and not the Jew-
> ish people alone . . . Hitler's regime cannot long
> survive without a war of revenge against France,
> Poland, Czechoslovakia . . . and against Soviet Rus-
> sia. Germany will not go to war today for she is not
> ready, but she is preparing for the morrow . . . Who
> knows; perhaps only four or five years, if not less,
> stand between us and that awful day.

Then he added:

> In this period — the four or five years remaining —
> we must double our numbers, for the size of the Jew-
> ish population on that day may determine our fate
> at the post-war settlement.

Hitler's threat was showing in the mood and attitude of the
new immigrants. They were coming off the boats singing,
happy, and excited about a new chance for life with dignity.
The Arabs, of course, were bitter and angered by the danger

the newcomers posed. They viewed the ever increasing Jewish numbers as a threat to their existence — to their own dreams of an Arab State. The Arabs didn't even consider the many economic benefits that Jews brought with them. They blamed the British for opening the door to their enemies in Palestine. It was a mixture of jealousy and resentment that Arabs in the Middle East held against Europeans with their different culture, religion, and customs.

The resentment kept building until it broke into the open in April 1936. Two Jews were taken off a bus and murdered by Arabs. In retaliation, militant members of the Haganah murdered two Arabs near Petan Tikvah. Violence and attacks by Arabs followed in many parts of Palestine. Seventy Jews were killed in Jaffa, 74 in Tiberias, many in other cities and villages. Arab strike committees were formed in a number of cities. Haj Amin, the Grand Mufti, who was previously supported by the British, sensed the popular mood was turning against them and rather than lose his standing with his people he joined the strong anti-British movement. He visited Hitler in Berlin and was given a hero's welcome. The Arab resentment against the British was just as strong as it was against the Jews. Haj Amin became the Head of the Higher Arab Committee at the end of April and led a general strike. The Arab revolt spread during the summer of 1936. There was a battle between the British troops and the Arabs near Tulkarm. The intensity of Arab attacks on the roads increased.

Jews were now performing some of the work abandoned by Arab workers who joined the rebellion. Not all the Arabs were taking part in the rebellion, some remained at their jobs. The British did not react decisively. There was a lot of hesitation, and sometimes reluctance to deal firmly with the problem. It was partly caused by the insufficient number of British soldiers to deal with the situation. They were on the defensive and did not seriously attempt to break the rebellion. Even after they built up their forces substantially in August, it was clear that they preferred a peaceful solution. They began to sympathize with the Arabs in order to stop the rebellion. They didn't attempt to arrest the Grand Mufti although it was clear that he was a key Arab rebellion leader.

To pacify the Arabs, the British cut Jewish immigration sharply. They cut the quotas deeply, causing the number of Jewish immigrants in 1936 to drop to about 30,000, less than half of the 1935 number. There was more bad news for Jews. The British Foreign Office began to play an increasingly important role in shaping Britain's foreign policy in the Middle East taking some of the key decision-making away from the Colonial Office. The Foreign Office had little interest in letting Jews have their own country. They were more interested in obtaining the goodwill of Arab rulers in the entire Middle East.

Anthony Eden, the British Foreign Secretary, depended on the advice of George Rendel from his Eastern Department. The British began to move toward satisfying Arab demands, which called for the cessation of the Jewish immigration, and in fact, for the scrapping of the entire idea of creating a Jewish National Home in Palestine.

All this came as a surprise to Abram and to many other Jews who got used to the relatively normal life during the years prior to 1936. In addition to the Arab danger and the prevailing feeling of uncertainty, the economic situation had worsened. The construction industry which had been booming slowed down and then came to a virtual halt. Abram and his people couldn't get a single contract and his group disbanded. For a while, Abram could not get any work whatsoever. There was no social security, no unemployment benefits; there wasn't a single agency that could help. Abram's emotions were now in real turmoil. There he was, successful, sending money to his family in Poland every month, and suddenly he couldn't even feed himself. For six weeks he had little to eat; there was a period of several days when he ate nothing, not even a piece of bread. He was too proud to ask his relatives for help. He was roaming the streets of Tel Aviv looking for any kind of work, but to no avail. One day he ran into a friend who was also a construction worker. The man looked at Abram's face, said, "You didn't eat, did you?" and took him to a cheap eating place. Finally, because of his reputation as an expert builder, he started getting a little work here and there.

With the Arab revolt in full swing, the Haganah was desperately trying to protect the Jews. They didn't have enough people to even think of any offensive, they were just trying to save Jewish lives. Abram was given an assignment to guard Jewish homes in Jaffa and other places. After the wave of surprise Arab attacks in April and May of 1936, Haganah became more efficient in protecting their people and there were relatively few Jewish casualties. Yet Haganah was still in its infancy without real knowledge of training methods and weaponry. They were learning as they went along.

Orde Charles Wingate served as an intelligence officer in Palestine from 1936 to 1939. He was a very unconventional man. At first he helped the Jews because he believed deeply in the Bible and considered them as the rightful owners of the Holy Land. As he got involved in the affairs of the Jews in Palestine, he saw what they had accomplished with the previously owned Palestinian land. He saw the progress Jews brought to agriculture, in the building of new cities, and he became a Zionist at heart. Wingate initiated Wingate's Commandos and brought discipline to his Jewish trainees, and showed them how to use imagination and the element of surprise. He would hit Jews he thought too slow in following his orders, pushing them, exhorting them to do better. He told them, "This is your land; fight for it."

Abram finally was able to get a full-time job as a garage mechanic. He decided there was no future for him in construction. Again, he started from the bottom, and was a quick learner. He bought English books about cars, engines, etc., which helped him to learn the English language. One day the garage manager came to Abram and said, "I must confess to you; I really don't understand the transmission differential. I see you read books about it. Will you explain that to me?" Abram did and shortly after he made Abram his assistant. One day a man by the name of Sonin took Abram to the side and told him that he was one of the liaison men between Wingate and the Haganah. He told Abram that Wingate needed a few men like him because of his mechanical ability. Abram was flattered because Wingate was accepting into his training program only men who really knew Israel well, knew the roads, who spoke Arabic and were completely dependable. Abram told Sonin he was very interested, but that he wanted to visit Poland first. His brother, Moniek, was sick (he hadn't been told that Moniek had actually died of a heart attack). Abram thought that by going to Poland, he could help his family come to Palestine. Before the end of 1937, he found out about Moniek's death. He went by boat to Alexandria and from there to Poland. Upon his arrival he could immediately tell how much the situation of the Jews in Poland had deteriorated. There were signs everywhere, on every wall, every fence, "Jews to Palestine," "Boycott Jewish Stores," "Beat Jews."

His parents wanted to leave, but the British tightened the immigration rules considerably. As far as the British were concerned, the Silbersteins could not be admitted because they were too young to be supported, yet could not get jobs on their own. Grandfather Noah was sick, confined to bed, and couldn't go, and Chaim couldn't leave because he had to take care of him.

Abram became sick at heart of the poisonous atmosphere in Poland, and couldn't wait to be back in Palestine. Now he appreciated his opportunities for the future in his new home even more although the situation looked bleak at the moment. Upon his arrival back in Palestine he contacted Sonin and soon became a full-fledged member of the Wingate Commandos. He had a short meeting with Wingate himself at a kibbutz.

Wingate wanted to know how much Abram knew about weapons and the countryside. Under Wingate he went through regular army training, jumping over obstacles, learned bayonet fighting, and how to best use rifles.

Abram thought Wingate was a little crazy, but he was fascinated by him. He was eagerly learning what Wingate and the three British sergeants who were helping him were trying to teach the Jews about how to fight the Arabs. Arabs would almost always attack at night, in groups of 200 or 300. They were mostly Palestinians, but some were Transjordanians. The Syrians, and Lebanese would also come over and attack Jewish settlements and towns.

The Jews would wait in their positions until the Arabs came close and then would open fire. Most of the time that caused the Arabs to flee. In Abram's first military engagement the Arabs did some shooting, but only succeeded in killing an Arab cook who was working for the Jews. The Arabs fled after a short firefight. The second engagement took place at Tabaria. Abram, in the dark of the night, shot at Arab silhouettes about 30–40 yards away, but never got involved in hand-to-hand combat. This simply wasn't the Arabs' style of fighting. They would come close to the Jewish lines, but that was as far as it went. They were mostly peasants, uneducated, and poorly trained. The training and general orientation of the Jews was now far superior. The Arabs began to concentrate their efforts in ambushing Jewish vehicles on the roads.

Wingate, because of his Zionist views, began having trouble with his superiors. They decided to ship him out to Eritrea in Africa and he never came back. Orde Wingate never got his secret wish to become the Commander of the future Jewish Army. But, he was very helpful in creating the foundation for the Jewish Army, and thereby was quite instrumental in establishing the future State of Israel.

In spite of all the suspicions of his military superiors, Wingate was a great British patriot and a brilliant imaginative soldier. From January to May of 1941, he led an Ethiopian force, accompanied by Emperor Haile Selassie, and took the capital of Addis Ababa back from the Italian conquerors. Then he was sent to India; he organized the "Chindits" and later helped organize and train the U.S. "Merrill's Marauders" commanded by Frank Merrill. In 1943 his Chindits entered Japanese-held Burma and played havoc with Japanese supply lines. He rose to Major General and led the airborne troops invading central Burma in March of 1944. He succeeded in severing the important Mandalay to Myitkyina railway, but soon afterward was killed in an airplane crash. Orde Wingate is one of Israel's great heroes and is still admired by many all over the world for his courage and ingenuity.

Abram, with the experience of defending fellow Jews from the Arab revolt under his belt, matured in many ways. This young man who came to Palestine only because of his father's wishes was then, at best, uncertain about his future. He became good at organizing people and things. He was a talented artist, and most of all a truly great human being. Abram was honest to a fault; a fighter for his convictions; courageous to a degree that some might consider foolish; straight as an arrow in his thinking and behavior, sometimes even bordering on naiveté. In Poland he was totally frustrated because he knew that a young Jew had nothing to look forward to but hate and abuse, physical as well as psychological, from his Polish neighbors; a denial of study in schools of higher learning; and most of all, the continuous threat to his and his family's well-being and even life. In Poland Zionism was far from his mind, yet after his arrival in Palestine something magical happened. The enthusiasm, the feeling of building a new country, the freedom from fear and scorn and hate was very infectious. Abram was swept up by it and surrendered to it body and soul. The danger from the Arabs was a minor obstacle to those young people full of zeal and fire in their hearts. At long last they had found a home. Fighting the Arabs and the English only hardened them. All their energies were now being released, and they fully relished it. Abram felt like a real man now and enjoyed dating, but that was still secondary in his priorities. Building a new and exciting life was, by far, more important.

A royal commission headed by Lord Peel began to study the Palestine situation and reported their findings in July 1937. The report outlined the diametrically opposed desires of both Jews and Arabs to have their own country in Palestine, and concluded that Britain's obligations to the two opposing sides were irreconcilable. It therefore recommended the partition of the country and the abandonment of the Mandate. Even though this was the first time that a British official commission spoke of creating a Jewish State, of adding new areas to the Jewish holdings, involving moving many Arabs from their homes, the Zionists were not fully satisfied because of limits placed on Jewish immigration as well as other factors. The Arabs were horrified by the very idea of a Jewish State in their midst and by a suggested forcible movement of part of their population from their homes. Because of this the Arab revolt broke out again in the fall of 1937. On September 26, 1937, Lewis Andrews, one of the top British officials, was assassinated by the Arabs. This was the straw that broke the camel's back. The British Foreign Office that until then had pretty much dictated the government policy in the Middle East, now had to let the Army do its job. The military finally got the green light and dealt forcibly with the Arab rebellion. They removed the Grand Mufti from his position as the Head of the Supreme Arab Council, and gave orders to arrest the leaders of the Arab revolt. The Grand Mufti was now afraid of the British and what they might do to him personally and, dressed in Bedouin clothes, he escaped to Lebanon. He never returned to Palestine but still continued to fight for his cause even though his influence had been greatly diminished.

However, even without the Mufti's leadership, the Arab rebellion spread into a full-fledged revolt and lasted to the end of

1938. The British fought it with capital punishment of captured offenders and even collective punishment of entire Arab villages. Even with these measures the revolt continued unabated; the British could use all the help they could get. They started using the Haganah, even though it was still officially illegal, for offensive operations. Haganah formed Special Night Squads that worked closely with the British Army. The training, which the British were now providing for the Haganah and other Jewish groups, later boomeranged against them when the Jews themselves rebelled against them after World War II. Many Jews, especially the younger ones, became very frustrated with the continuous changes of British policy in Palestine. This frustration was greatly increased by what Hitler was doing to Jews under his control in Germany, Austria, and Czechoslovakia even before the outbreak of the war. They didn't agree with Haganah's policy of trying to work with the British. New revisionist militant groups were being formed which joined the Irgun Zvai Leumi. They became increasingly resentful of the Haganah, and wanted an all out war against the Arabs who were attacking Jewish settlements and towns. In June 1938 the British hanged a young revisionist who was caught shooting at an Arab bus. In July the Irgun exploded mines in a fruit market in Haifa, killing 74 and wounding 129, virtually all Arabs. The majority of the Jewish community condemned the killings, but many began questioning Haganah's policies as too conciliatory.

The British government, as it had done many times before, again changed its policy in Palestine. They held the London Conference to deal with the future of this land. It was attended by representatives of five Arab countries, Palestinian Arabs, the Zionist Executive, and the hosts as well. The Palestinian Arabs refused to meet directly with the Jews, but there were a few conferences attended by some of the leaders of the Arab countries and the Zionists. The London Conference produced no positive results and broke up in disagreement. After its conclusion, another White Paper was issued by the British in May, 1939.

This paper was a blow to all Zionist hopes and aspirations. It called for an independent "Palestinian State" but under its provisions Jewish immigration would be limited to 75,000 in five years which would give the Arabs a great majority in the new State. It gave the Jews and Arabs certain veto powers which, in effect, would make it impossible for the new State to function altogether. Skeptics considered the White Paper to be a duplicitous formula which would allow the British to continue to rule Palestine and thereby secure their position in the entire Middle East. They obviously took a page from Julius Caesar's "divide and conquer" policy. Jews, particularly the more militant ones, lost all confidence in British promises as held out by the Balfour Declaration. Many of them were now seriously thinking that it would take a "Jewish rebellion" to accomplish their dream of a National Jewish Home. Even the Arabs were unhappy with the White Paper. They wanted an Arab Palestinian State with no conditions attached. The Jews now began to look at illegal immigration as the only way to increase their strength and improve their position.

~ 4 ~

A BRITISH SOLDIER
IN FRANCE

All this was changed by the outbreak of World War II. Hitler rejected all pleas from European governments to settle his demands on Poland, and German soldiers began their assault on Poland in the early morning hours of September 1, 1939. In spite of their lingering hopes of saving peace, the people of Europe finally came to a conclusion that Hitler was determined to rule them and perhaps the world. The only way to stop him was by force of arms. A heartbroken Chamberlain, who just a year earlier came home from Munich triumphantly waving a piece of paper signed by Adolf Hitler, declaring "peace in our time," was forced to take into his War Cabinet his foremost critic, Winston Churchill, who for years had been warning his countrymen of Hitler's threat. The British, most of whom considered Churchill an adventurer, now welcomed him with a sigh of relief as the new First Lord of the Admiralty. Chamberlain remained the Prime Minister until May 10, 1940, when even his conservative friends abandoned him and he was forced to resign. He died a few months later still finding it hard to accept his own gullibility.

In Palestine, Hitler's quick conquest of Poland in September 1939, and the lack of any offensive by the combined British-French army caused a fundamental change in the Jewish attitude toward the British. They could see that Hitler and his racial policy threatened the very existence of the European Jewry that was almost the sole source of people and money needed to build a Jewish State.

Even the Irgun, which was responsible for terrorist attacks against the British, radically changed its policy and worked closely with them. Irgun's spiritual father, Vladimir Zabotinsky, died in 1940 and was replaced by David Raziel, who himself was killed in action in May 1941. However, the most militant members of the Irgun were still against any cooperation with the British, whom they considered treacherous, and broke away from the Irgun. They formed an extreme terrorist organization, Lehi, which the British called "the Stern Gang" because of the name of its founder, Abraham Stern. Abraham Stern now took a step which most of his contemporaries considered as crazy. He sent a messenger, Naphtali Lubentchick, to Beirut in order to contact the German Consul in Ankara, Turkey, and through him to propose a deal with Hitler. The Lehi would do its best to assist the Germans in conquering Palestine, if Hitler agreed to the creation of a Jewish pro-German State, and help the transfer of European Jews to the Jewish State.

Abraham Stern's ideas were, perhaps, not completely crazy. He was much more pessimistic about Jewish survival under Hitler than virtually all his contemporaries who could not bring themselves to believe that the very lives of their Jewish brethren in Europe were in mortal danger. He hated the British, and could see that Hitler was willing to make deals with anybody, as long as it served his goals. After all, wasn't communism the fascists' worst enemy — that didn't stop Hitler from making a deal with Stalin.

Nothing came out of this attempt anyway; Lubentchick was arrested by the British on his way to Beirut. Stern himself was considered too dangerous even by the Jewish leadership. Both the Haganah and the Irgun helped the British police to find his hiding place, and he was shot dead while British soldiers attempted to take him into custody. Stern's contemporaries — friends and enemies — were not the only ones that took him seriously. Even today some Israelis think that his ideas had merit and remember him as a hero.

The main body of Palestine Jews, however, clearly understood that their survival depended on the British being able to defeat Hitler and did everything in their power to help them. Ben-Gurion became the most prominent Jewish leader in Palestine. He bitterly opposed the British on the White Paper and many of their other policies, clearly understood the need to help the British in defeating Hitler and worked hard to create a Jewish armed force which could defend Palestine.

All these events profoundly changed the lives of Jews in Palestine. Abram always had bad premonitions about Hitler's plans for Jews and couldn't stop thinking about his family in Poland and what was happening to them. The following is an excerpt from the book *The Companies of Jewish Volunteers in the Royal Army Service Crops (R.A.S.C.) in World War II, 1939–1945;* Volume I, page 40. This chapter was written by Mr. Tzvi Atlas who, after the creation of the State of Israel, became a prominent official in the Ministry of Defense and later in the Ministry of Health:

> At the start of World War II in September 1939, I was with a group of friends from the Haganah in the special force created by Captain Wingate called S.N.S. (Special Night Squad). Our camp was located in the Arabic school in Tiberias. I lived with several friends in the same room. One of them was Abram S[ilberstein].
>
> I had a radio that transmitted the Voice of Jerusalem to us. Although it was an old radio, we still could receive radio programming from many other

countries. Abraham [*sic*] S. returned from night duty around the hot springs of Tiberias. We all sat down discussing various subjects. Suddenly Abraham heard, to our big surprise, a Polish station. And the shock was that we heard a voice of the Mayor of Hrubieszow asking urgently for medical help, bandages, bed sheets, etc.

The Mayor, without trying to conceal his crying, said that he does not know how long the city will stand up to the attack, as the Germans are advancing quickly, and that their paratroops were being dropped in the nearby fields.

Abraham was terribly touched and excited. He said, "My family is there, and I must try and save them. I am going to enlist into the British Army. I must fight."

The town Hrubieszow was the town where Abraham lived prior to his immigration to Palestine. At that time we still couldn't enlist, and we had to carry on with our normal guard duties of the S.N.S., although we already knew that the unit will be disbanded within weeks. The British ordered Capt. Wingate back to England while the unit was hastily moved to an army camp near Aco.

Officially the S.N.S. was a police force attached to the Staffordshire Infantry Regiment. That was a way of concealing the truth. In fact, it was an infantry fighting unit. The reason for the concealment was to mislead the Arabs who brought up the subject in the Parliament. Ten days later, with the help of a letter from one of the officers, Abram managed to enlist into the Royal Army Service Corps, a British Transport Unit.

Before getting approval, Abram had to have a thorough physical examination. He was declared in good shape. He went back to the officer who sent him to a commissary where they issued him a British Army uniform. Abram was now officially a member of the Transport Unit of the Staffordshire Regiment. He was the first Palestine Jew to become a British soldier.

Abram was excited; he had a new mission in life: to fight the evil that threatened to destroy everything he loved and all his dreams for the future. They assigned a truck to him, and he made friends among his fellow soldiers. He was eagerly learning English using a dictionary. He was the only Jew in his unit, but somehow he felt at home. An English soldier saw him studying the dictionary and asked him to help him write a letter to his family. This made Abram feel good.

One day, during inspection, a sergeant noticed how shiny Abram's shoes were. He was impressed and said, "I would like you to shine my shoes like that." This didn't sit well with Abram. He said, "No disrespect, but I'm not shining anybody's shoes, not even the King's." The sergeant was taken aback. "No, no, it's all right." Abram's first reaction to the request was that, perhaps, the sergeant asked him for a shoeshine because he was a Jew. He was too proud to comply. His fellow soldiers explained to him that it was stupid of him to refuse, that in the British Army it is considered an honor to be selected by a sergeant to clean his shoes. They started to tease him: "Now you are done; you are finished."

Abram now understood that he had made a mistake, but it was too late to undo it. A couple of days later Abram was told to report to the office. The soldiers were laughing; they thought that Abram might have to spend a few days in the brig for insubordination. In the Orderly Room, an officer was waiting for him. He said, "Private Silberstein, you are promoted to Lance Corporal." Apparently the sergeant appreciated Abram's spirit and independence and suggested the promotion. Abram went to the sergeant to thank him. The man, who was a Scotsman, said, "Silberstein, you know sweet fuck-all about the British Army, but you will make a bloody good N.C.O." He put Abram in charge of an all-British platoon of about 60 men. Abram was stunned. His fellow soldiers were impressed by this unexpected turn of events. Abram bought them drinks to celebrate the occasion, and they all had a good time laughing and joking.

Abram was put in charge of driving a number of trucks to the Syrian border, having them loaded with supplies and bringing them back to his unit's warehouse. He was with the Staffordshire Regiment for about six weeks when he heard that the British were forming a new unit of volunteers to be sent to France. The unit was to consist of Arabs only. Prisoners in British jails that were serving sentences for murder, theft, and other crimes were being offered pardons if they joined the new unit. There were supposed to be 700 men in the unit, but only 400 Arabs volunteered. The British decided to fill the quota by letting volunteer Jews join the unit. Abram felt that staying with his regiment in Palestine was not what he was looking for. He was consumed by a passionate desire to fight the enemy.

He knew that the majority of the new unit were Arab criminals, but he felt he could handle them. Abram was promoted to sergeant and was put in charge of about fifty men, all Arabs. The Jewish volunteers were educated and highly motivated. The Arabs were illiterate criminals who were there only because they thought this was better than jail. Strangely, after a short while a certain comradeship in arms developed and the Jews and Arabs got along fairly well. The men in the new unit received their basic training in Palestine. During the passage there were sea-storms and virtually all the men in the unit got sick. Abram was lucky, he took it well. They disembarked in Marseille and were put on a horse-transport train that took them to Rennes in Brittany. Their commanding officer was a Major Keytor who happened to be the British Queen's cousin.

Soon after their arrival Major Keytor and his men were given the task of building a new rail supply line to the front in the East. Another unit, which was all British, was putting in a parallel line a little bit to the south. Abram's unit, the 401 A.M.P.C. British Expeditionary Forces, had virtually all Jewish

N.C.O.s. All were eager to contribute to the war effort. Their work was progressing rapidly, and after two weeks they were way ahead of the line being placed by the all-British unit.

One day a number of British soldiers from the other unit came over. They were very upset with this bunch of foreigners making them look bad. They carried big sticks and were clearly looking for a fight. Their leader said, "We didn't come here to finish this bloody war in one week." They were threatening to break Major Keytor's men's necks if they continued to do their work so fast. It was an ugly confrontation. Abram's people defended themselves saying that they were taking seriously their responsibility to finish the job as soon as possible. Somehow a brawl was avoided and the British left.

Abram felt good. He was happy to play a part in the war. He was anxious to get into battle, to do more, but in the meantime, he was concentrating on his work and on training his platoon. He felt physically very strong and was driving his men hard to make them better soldiers. Strangely, with all their background of hostility towards the Jews, the Arabs in his platoon responded well. They couldn't help but develop a certain admiration for this man who was clearly hell-bent on shaping them into a top-notch fighting unit.

One day while training his men, Abram suddenly broke into loud laughter. The thought occurred to him of how ridiculous this situation was. There he was, a Polish Jew, an immigrant to Palestine, a sergeant in the British Army, using the English language to train Arab criminals on how to fight the Germans. He kept laughing and laughing. He just couldn't stop. The Arabs around him were puzzled. What happened to their leader? Had he finally gone nuts?

The "phony war" on the Western front continued. The English and French on one side and the Germans on the other hardly ever exchanged a shot. Abram wanted to see action; he was waiting for the front to explode. In the meantime, he had to be satisfied with doing the best he could. The Arabs were unhappy with the Army rations they were receiving. They often contained pork which their religion forbade them to eat. The Jews in Major Keytor's unit didn't have this problem. Most of them were not strongly religious and were quite satisfied with regular army food.

The French in Rennes were glad to have the military stationed in their town. The shopkeepers were ringing up extra sales; the prostitutes were doing a brisk business. It was cold; Abram and his soldiers slept in corrugated huts with cement floors. The men covered themselves with blankets at night, but many were catching colds. There were many wooden boxes abandoned near their camp, and Abram came up with an idea. He made a nested two-piece bed using the boxes. It looked good, so he had his men make beds for the whole platoon. A few British officers heard about the beds. They came, looked at them, were impressed and took photographs. They sent the photos to the War Office recommending that beds like these should be made whenever the boxes were available.

Abram became popular because of his inventiveness and was asked to make beds for the entire company. Major Keytor took a real liking to Abram. He was impressed by his spirit, his dedication, and ingenuity. The two became good friends. One day, Keytor said to Abram, "I would like you to go to England to meet my father. I want to show him a specimen of a Palestinian Jew. I also want to send him drawings of the beds you made." He arranged a week's leave for Abram. The Senior Keytor lived in London. He was a general in the British Army during World War I, now retired. He lived in posh surroundings in a large house at 11 Eaton Square. There were butlers, cooks, and maids in the house. The general was old and strict in his ways. He kept Abram at his side for seven days, curious about what was going on in the Middle East. Abram was dying to see London, but the general kept him busy discussing things and gave him no time to see anything. Abram went back to his unit. For the next four months they were busy with the railway. Then suddenly everything around him collapsed.

From September 3, 1939, when Britain and France, having no other choice, declared war on Germany, until May 10, 1940, the "phony war" on the Western front was on. It seemed that Hitler wasn't too anxious to attack his enemies in the West and the English and French were also satisfied with the status quo. The British and French public's morale was low, unlike at the outset of World War I. Their leaders knew that they had let Hitler rearm Germany without a corresponding build-up of their own forces and were perhaps playing for time hoping to catch up. They also knew how an all-out war was abhorrent to their peoples after the massive bloodletting they suffered in 1914–1918.

However, all their hopes came crashing down when the German army opened its all-out attack on the Western Allies on May 10, 1940. Most people in the world were unaware to what degree Western governments had allowed the quality and quantity of their armed forces to deteriorate. They could not believe that in a few short years, Hitler could build a force far superior to those of his enemies.

The Germans surprised everyone with the power of their army. Not only were their soldiers better trained and motivated and their arms of higher quality, but they also used new military tactics which were far superior to the ones employed by the French and the British. After having broken through the enemy lines, the German mobile armored formations were ranging far behind the actual front lines causing havoc to their enemy's supply lines and demoralizing them. Their Stukas flew low, attacking military targets, as well as thousands of refugees on the roads causing further confusion and chaos.

The Germans surged across Belgium and swept into France. The British and French were in a disorderly retreat. The celebrated and supposedly impregnable Maginot Line, which took the French years to construct and perfect, collapsed with little or no resistance when attacked from both the east and the west. Hundreds of thousands of refugees were jamming the roads trying to escape, but the speed of the German advance left them behind. It was a rout, a catastrophe. The victorious invaders drove a deep wedge between the French and the British armies while taking hundreds of thousands of prisoners.

In a swift enveloping movement, they pushed the British Expeditionary Force toward the English Channel. The British abandoned their equipment, and were in a hasty retreat toward the sea hoping to just save their soldiers from being taken prisoner. The French army escaped toward the south. Their soldiers were completely demoralized. They put up a temporary resistance line on the Somme River, but the Germans broke through again, and in a matter of days Paris was occupied. The French people were crying in the streets of the French capital. They watched the hated Boche marching down the Champs-Elysee. It was all over for the French. On June 22 they got a bitter taste of defeat when, on Hitler's orders, the French generals came to sign a surrender. Hitler made sure that the signing took place in the very same railcar where the Germans surrendered in World War I on November 8, 1918. In a single stroke Hitler accomplished what the German Kaiser couldn't do in more than four years. Nightmare became reality. The madman became master of all Europe from the Soviet Union's western frontier to the Atlantic Ocean.

The situation of the British Expeditionary Force was precarious at best. It reached the English Channel at Dunkirk. In a hasty retreat, they left behind almost all of their tanks, trucks, guns, and other military equipment. Great Britain was now in danger of losing virtually their entire trained military force. Their 400,000 soldiers in France were the cream of their army. Now the big question was, would they be able to rescue them from becoming German prisoners?

To Abram, all this came as a shattering blow. All his hopes were based on the Western armies' ability to defeat Hitler. For days he was walking around in a daze. But this was no time for reflection. British officers started training Keytor's men in explosives. They trained them in laying mines behind their retreating units hoping to slow down the oncoming Germans and give their troops a little breathing time to organize a temporary line of resistance, so that they would be able to save most of their trapped men by evacuating them to England.

Keytor's unit, which was stationed quite a bit to the west of the mass of the encircled British, was moved further east, closer to the center of the surrounded British forces. The unit got orders to move eastward at daytime and back to the west at night. This went on for a couple of days. It was puzzling. Keytor's soldiers were given different looking helmets and parts of uniforms to wear every day. Abram and some of his friends in the unit thought that this was done to fool the French, and make them believe that new British reinforcements were being thrown into the fighting.

Keytor was given the task of destroying certain bridges and damaging the roads to slow down the German formations moving towards Brest Fortress on the west coast of France. It was also to lay mines on strategic crossroads. The pressure from the German army continued from all sides now, and Abram's unit eventually wound up in St. Malo, Normandy, south of Southampton on the other side of the channel. All the roads to St. Malo were cut off and they started calling and looking for small boats to evacuate them. The problem was that there was a shortage of boats and the all-British units were being given preference over those of other nationalities. The non-British were used to engage the Germans in rear guard action, in effect sacrificing themselves in order to give the regular British units time to escape. It was chaos. Abram still found it hard to believe how everybody misjudged the lack of power of the Allied armies. The British tanks were poorly made; the French guns were obsolete and had to be pulled by horses; their weapons were inferior. Abram's men were given anti-armor rifles which were almost impossible to handle because they were nearly twice the size of a normal rifle. The force of the recoil was so great that it hurt the soldiers when they were used. They had to use small sandbags to reduce the impact, and this greatly diminished the effectiveness of the rifles. The only good weapons they had were the Bren guns and Lewis light machine guns, but that wasn't nearly enough to match the equipment of the onrushing Germans.

They were in St. Malo twenty-four hours when they observed, just about a quarter mile further south, German tanks moving west attempting to cut off the remaining Allied units. German war planes were flying low, taking photographs, and attacking British units. New British troops came to St. Malo, but they were being evacuated leaving behind all their equipment. Abram's men were given orders to push the abandoned vehicles into the sea so as to prevent the Germans from capturing them. Finally, Keytor and his soldiers were the only ones remaining in St. Malo, cut off on all sides. The German planes were in the process of bombing a nearby installation. Abram and his soldiers kept pushing the equipment into the waters of the English Channel, desperately hoping for a boat to come and rescue the men.

Unexpectedly, a group of about 10 young French women appeared carrying armloads full of civilian clothing. They told Abram that they were prostitutes from the local brothel, and they wanted to save the soldiers from being taken prisoner. It was all very touching. The soldiers thanked them profusely and gave them some cigarettes and candy but refused to leave, still hoping for a boat to come to their rescue. Finally, a small old boat came in. There was just one old grizzly Englishman on it. The entire unit got in, but just barely, without any room to move around. There was a steam engine in the front and iron rods leading to the rudder. There wasn't enough room on the boat itself, so some of the men were standing on the iron rods. They left St. Malo at 7 o'clock in the evening.

The captain zigzagged trying to avoid German Stukas that were bombing and strafing many of the hundreds of boats ferrying British and other Allied soldiers to England. Most of these boats were privately owned and they came out, at tremendous risk to their owners' lives, to save their countrymen. Nothing like this had ever happened in the history of the world. Hundreds of boats, some so overweight that they barely stayed afloat, were moving slowly towards the English shore completely unprotected from the German Messerschmitts and Heinkels that were attacking them day and night. Abram saw a boat full of British soldiers that had left St. Malo before them, slowly sink into the waters of the Channel with soldiers desperately clinging to parts of the disappearing boat. Already greatly overweight, there was no question of Abram's boat helping. The old captain pleaded with them to throw their guns into the water, but they refused. They arrived in Southhampton at 4 o'clock in the morning.

～ 5 ～

ENGLAND

A few elderly English ladies were waiting for them at the South-hampton docks. They were very sweet and brought tea and cookies for the exhausted soldiers. These patriotic women were extremely solicitous and tried hard to lift the spirits of the men by consoling them, telling them all was not lost and that everything would turn out to be all right. This was very touching and made the men feel good — at least they were appreciated. But there was an atmosphere of crisis and there was no time to rest. They were marched off to Butlin's Holiday camp.

The camp, and others like it, was named after Butlin, an English businessman. He knew the English were shy by nature and before the war he built dance halls for single men and women. They all gathered in a hall, and when the orchestra started playing, the announcer would say, "Dance." The guests were expected, without knowing each other, to ask someone to dance. This was the beginning of many new and fruitful relationships. The camps, of course, were empty after the war started and were used to house soldiers who were rescued from the debacle in France. There was plenty of room and Abram and his men were able to get some rest and relax for the first time in weeks.

After spending two weeks in the Butlin camp, they were taken to Kimberly which was originally an artillery base.

There was a great shortage of weapons because most of the units which were evacuated from France abandoned all their equipment. Soldiers were being trained with wooden sticks instead of rifles. Keytor's men, with their light machine guns in good order, were among the very few British attachments with real weapons. Weapons were the key to the ability of the British to defend their beloved island. The shortage of weapons was so paramount, it became the subject of most conversations. Abram remembers an English lady proudly telling him that her husband was promoted — he had been moved to stand next to the man with a real rifle.

After two weeks of training in Kimberly, Keytor received orders to move his unit to a position about 1 kilometer from the shores of the English Channel, directly south of London. They were placed in trenches which were dug out before they got there. They were given the responsibility of defending about one mile of the coastline in the event of German landings. There were five rows of anti-tank ditches in front of them. Wooden palisades were dug into the ditches. Keytor's men stayed in their positions for about three months, sleeping in the ditches, but the weather was fairly warm, so that was not a problem. The food was good and most of the talking was about how to fight the Germans in the event of an invasion. The English were putting up defensive balloons, and German planes were flying over taking photos without any interference.

In September the unit was ordered back to Kimberly. German planes were bombing London and Abram and his men were helping to pull corpses and survivors from the wreckage and removing the debris. The Jewish and Arab soldiers got along very well, working hand-in-hand trying to save peoples' lives. Keytor maintained strict discipline, and made them continue their training whenever time permitted.

The English were taking the hard times well. They knew

they were fighting for their lives, but that didn't cause them to lose their well-known sense of humor. A shop was hit by a bomb and had its entire front missing. The owner put up a sign, "We are open for business, even more than usual." In France the Germans had proven their superiority in the quality of their weapons, as well as in the leadership of their generals, and the English found it hard to swallow. The British fighters, although inferior in numbers, were giving the Luftwaffe a hard time. The "Battle of Britain" continued to rage during July, August, and into early September. The British knew that if the Luftwaffe was able to destroy their air force, it would have been much easier for the Germans to establish a bridgehead in England itself. Given the great shortage of arms to defend itself, England's very survival was at stake. A relatively small number of British and Allied fighter pilots, exhausted and with very little sleep, were sacrificing their lives to save their country, their homes and, their families. Winston Churchill, who took over as Prime Minister from the ailing, confused, heartbroken Chamberlain, said, "Never in the field of human conflict was so much owed by so many to so few."

After hundreds of air battles, an impatient Hitler made a grave, strategic mistake. The British had few planes left, even fewer pilots, and who knows what would have happened had the Luftwaffe continued to concentrate their attack on airfields and radar installations. Even though the Germans had sustained grave losses, they still enjoyed a numerical superiority. Incredibly, Hitler himself came to Britain's rescue. Frustrated by not achieving the complete control of the air quickly, he decided to punish the stubborn English by massive bombings of England's cities. This cost the English many lives and caused much destruction, but it gave the exhausted Air Fighter Command time to rest and to rebuild its strength. Seeing that he was not able to break Britain's spirit and with the weather worsening during the fall season, Hitler called off "Operation Sea Lion" as the projected invasion of England was called. Instead,

he cast his long glance towards the East and started prepara-
tions for the conquest of his recent partner, the Soviet Union.
He felt confident that, having destroyed the Western Allies'
armies in the west, and having secured his position there, he
would have no trouble defeating the Soviet Army in the east
without having to worry about a second front. The inept Soviet
invasion of Finland, with a population of only three million,
gave him additional reassurance that the Soviet army was weak
and poorly led.

The apparent abandonment of Hitler's plans to invade England gave Churchill and the British people time to breathe
and to rebuild their shattered army. Churchill knew that he
had a long road ahead of him. He said to the British people:

> Even though large tracts of Europe and many old
> and famous States have fallen or may fall into the
> grip of the Gestapo and all the odious apparatus of
> Nazi rule, we shall not flag or fail. We shall go on to
> the end, we shall fight in France, we shall fight in the
> seas and oceans, we shall fight with growing confi-
> dence and growing strength in the air, we shall de-
> fend our island, whatever the cost may be, we shall
> fight on the beaches, we shall fight on the landing-
> grounds, we shall fight in the fields and in the
> streets, we shall fight in the hills; we shall never sur-
> render, and even if, which I do not for a moment be-
> lieve, this island or a large part of it were subjugated
> and starving, then our Empire beyond the seas,
> armed and guarded by the British Fleet, would carry
> on the struggle, until, in God's good time, the New
> World, with all its power and might, steps forth to
> the rescue and the liberation of the Old.

All these momentous events caused Abram a great deal of
worry and uncertainty. He didn't know what was happening to

his family in Poland, but knew that they were in grave danger. Palestine was far away, but his heart was there with his young friends who were trying so hard to build a homeland of their own, and whose future was now being threatened by Hitler and his armies. He ached to be able to do more to fight the Nazis, but he was helpless, stymied by events completely beyond his control.

On their last day in London, Abram and his soldiers received a pleasant surprise, a parade in their honor was arranged. The reason was simply because they came back from France with all their weapons. Lord Gott, the Colonial Minister, greeted them at the parade. He came over to Abram and talked to him for a while. Abram and his men were very happy to be so appreciated.

The next day Abram's 401 A.M.P.C., B.E.F. was taken by train to Glasgow and boarded a ship departing for the Middle East. Abram was elated. He was going to be closer to home and would get a chance to fight the Nazis. It was late October 1940. The passage through Gibraltar was blocked so the ships had to take the route that went around the South African Cape. (They were part of a thirty-two ship convoy.) Abram was on a ship named *The Andes,* which was at one time a luxury liner. In addition to about 7,000 British troops on *The Andes,* there was also a field hospital. The convoy was guarded by battleships, destroyers, frigates, and other warships. They zigzagged as they were passing west of Brest. The convoy was attacked by German submarines; two of the ships were sunk, and several thousand soldiers were drowned. The convoy docked at Sierra Leone first, and stayed there for twenty-four hours. They tried to stop at Durbin, South Africa, but couldn't because of rough seas. They arrived in Capetown about four weeks after leaving Scotland and stayed there for about ten days.

An Australian convoy was also in port. The town was full of British and Australian soldiers. The bars and whorehouses were packed. Everybody was very merry; happy to be there after a long and dangerous voyage. The Australians were boisterous but friendly. One day while Abram was walking the streets of Capetown, he had to rub his eyes to make sure that what he was seeing was real. There was an Australian soldier standing in a street intersection directing traffic. He was completely naked.

Abram and some of the other Jews in his outfit were invited by local Jewish families into their homes. They were greeted warmly, enjoyed great hospitality and home cooked meals, but had to sleep on *The Andes*. After a week or so, they were ordered to board *The Andes* and departed, grateful for the opportunity to rest and the warm treatment they had received. The convoy went past Madagascar, a large island off the east coast of Africa, through the Persian Gulf, past the Red Sea, and to the Suez Canal. The Italian Army was holding Eritrea, so the convoy was forced to maneuver back and forth to avoid gunfire from Italian shore artillery. Finally, they disembarked at the Port of Suez and were taken by truck to Camp Genifa. It was early December 1940.

∼ 6 ∼

THE SUICIDE COMMANDO

At the Genifa base, there were two separate commando units — the 51st M.E. and the 52nd M.E. They came from different places and had different purposes. One volunteer group was under Major Keytor and it consisted of 180 men — sixty were English; seventy, Arabs; and fifty, Jews. The leader of the other group was Randolph Churchill (Winston's son). The training program was brutal; it included 50 kilometer marches in the desert without food or water; marches to the Great Bitter Lake (very salty); swimming across the lake loaded down with weapons; and running through obstacles that were extremely dangerous. One of the British officers said to Abram, "We want to make real supermen of you." They were being trained to handle camels and ride them at full gallop. They slept in tents and were busy all day receiving instructions and training. Not all of the men could stand the rigorous course; many dropped out.

One day Major Keytor came to their quarters and announced that a new, special command unit was being formed, which would be used for very dangerous missions and that it would require even tougher training. Abram's heart jumped for joy. Keytor told his soldiers that serving in this new unit would be extremely dangerous and only volunteers would be accepted. Abram's response was instant. He was the first to volunteer. Many of the soldiers under Abram liked him, admired his leadership qualities, and most of them volunteered as well.

The English officers also liked him. They were impressed by his spirit, his readiness to do anything asked of him, and his intense desire to get into heavy action. One night — it was almost morning — a Lieutenant Watson, who had taken a real liking to Abram, woke him, told him to be quiet, and whispered, "Silberstein, in about thirty minutes, forty men will be sent out on a mission. I don't believe any of them will ever come back. You are on the list. Do whatever you have to to get out of this mission." Abram told him that this was the kind of action he was waiting for, and that dodging it would be unfair to the others. Watson insisted, "I don't want you to go." Abram was equally determined. He said, "Thank you, Lieutenant Watson, but I must go." The Lieutenant punched the unsuspecting Abram and knocked him out. Abram regained consciousness a few minutes later. He could hardly contain his excitement. Finally, his dreams were coming true. He would be able to fight the hated Nazi soldiers.

A truck was waiting and took the forty men onto a desert road which ran through Mina House to Alexandria. Abram and a Sergeant Watts were in command. The commando boarded a large ship, *The Midway*. The letters of the name *Midway* were erased for security reasons. There was quite a fleet of gun boats around her as well as two small submarines. Everything had an aura of great importance. This was a mothership for submarines, and it had a section where the torpedoes were assembled and stored.

They were quartered next to the submarine crews who, after twenty-one days of sea operations, had returned to *The Midway* for a rest. The crews of the little subs were very friendly toward Abram's soldiers. There was no walking space in the tiny subs and the submariners used the opportunity to exercise their legs by taking frequent walks on *Midway*'s decks.

Abram's commando kept up its daily training in order to stay fit. Every morning a boat took them ashore and they ran for 12 kilometers even in the worst weather. For the first time they were introduced to the tommy gun, and it was not easy to master the art of assembling its enormously strong steel spring. Abram and Sergeant Watts demonstrated to the curious submarine crews how to use this weapon. In turn, the submariners would take Abram and his men down into the uncomfortable little submarines and show them how the little boats were operated.

The food on *The Midway* was excellent, a vast improvement over the Army rations. They enjoyed fresh eggs, butter, cheese, and bread. It was a real paradise. They spent two weeks on *The Midway*. Abram was trying to figure out what kind of mission Lieutenant Watson was talking about, but to no avail.

One day before the end of December 1940, Captain Keymer called them in for a meeting. He produced aerial maps of the North African coast and showed them the position of the opposing armies. He pointed out a 4 inch water pipeline parallel to a paved road running from Buq-Buq towards Bardia and Solum. The sands were constantly shifting and because of that the pipes were visible in some spots. They were important because, even though the water was salty, there was no other water available in the area. The pipelines were the only source of potable water available to the enemy in that area. The commando's mission would be to get ashore into enemy territory and blow up the pipeline.

The next morning they were transferred to a small Australian frigate named *Voyager* which took them down the Mediterranean coast. There were many alerts because of enemy planes flying overhead and they had to take cover frequently. On one occasion, they were bombed by four Italian planes that were flying at a high level, but all the bombs fell

into the sea. They didn't go ashore that night; they waited another twenty-four hours, and again nothing had happened.
Keymer spent all his time with the ship's Captain getting information over the radio.

They received new orders, and it was on an early evening in
February, 1941, when Abram and his men left the *Voyager* in
small row boats. They reached the Mediterranean shore at
West Solum and climbed a 300 meter cliff leading to a flat top.
After they reached the top of the cliff four Italian planes flying
overhead spotted them. The soldiers hit the ground looking
for cover. They found themselves in an open-air army field
latrine. The smell was terrible, but it was the only place they
could find, and they dove into it. They were covered by feces up
to their necks. The planes were flying very low now, circling,
looking for them. They dropped incendiary bombs to light up
the area. Captain Keymer shouted, "I will shoot anyone who
moves." They stayed in their position until the Italian planes finally gave up and left. The soldiers went down the cliff back to
the seashore to wash the feces off. They dipped into the sea
fully dressed and with their equipment and arms. Cleaning was
not easy. The pervasive smell stayed with them for a long time.

Dawn came. Still in the water, they spotted a row of caves
just below the cliff. They decided the caves would provide great
shelter. They were beautiful, carved out of soft rock by the Italians. Keymer decided to stay there and wait for orders. As soon
as they had settled down, heavy artillery fire started, and shells
were flying over their heads and into the little port of Solum.
The firing, coming from the desert, was a clear indication that
the British Army had bypassed Solum. The enemy, while retreating, was trying to destroy the port installations by using its
artillery. The following morning the commandos were told to
proceed to the port area in order to unload a small British ammunition ship. The orders were to unload it as quickly as it was
humanly possible. The soldiers were eager to do the job and
worked like crazy. Heavy boxes of ammunition began to pile up

on the small jetty. Abram suddenly noticed that his money and wallet were missing. He told his men to carry on, that he would be back in a few minutes. He ran up to the cave and found his wallet. As he was leaving, he was thrown back into the cave by the impact of a terrific explosion. At that very moment, Italian planes started bombing the ship at the jetty. He ran down and found the place in shambles; bodies and limbs were strewn all over the jetty. The carnage was terrible.

The upper deck of the ship had been hit, but it was still afloat. They moved all the wounded to its deck and the ship proceeded to Alexandria. None of the wounded survived the trip. The commando lost twenty-one men. Abram buried seven men near the road above Solum. This was a temporary burial; they had orders to bury their dead near the road and to mark the mileage. One of the dead was Abram's partner, Sergeant Watts. He buried him with half a bottle of whiskey that Watts always kept in his pocket. While they were digging the graves, shells were falling nearby, but caused no new casualties.

Abram was left with eighteen men. They returned to the cave, blood-stained from carrying their wounded; they all stunk of dried blood. They stayed in the cave for twenty-four hours. No one spoke a word. They were in shock, and the stench of blood stayed with them.

The next morning, while they were in the cave trying to recover from the disastrous bombing, two dispatch riders found them and brought new orders. An Italian brigade of 4,000 soldiers and officers signaled that it was willing to surrender to the advancing British. They were told to march to a certain milepost of the desert road. Abram and his men were given four trucks and ordered to meet the Italians, strip them of their weapons, and load these onto the trucks. They were told to be careful in case some of the Italian soldiers, unhappy with the surrender, would start shooting at them. To play it safe, they took up a defensive posture ready to open fire if necessary. After a couple of hours, small dots began to appear on the hori-

zon. The dots got larger and larger, and finally, they saw thousands of Italian soldiers coming in. It was an incredible sight.
Most of them appeared to suffer from dysentery, and their legs
were covered by feces and by blood. The smell was overpower-
ing. Men were begging for water, crying, "Aqua, aqua." Abram's
heart went out to the poor men, but they were short of water
themselves. He told the Italians to hold out just a little longer,
that water was on the way. The Italians were ordered to lay
down their weapons in a few designated places from which
Abram and his men were loading them onto the four trucks.
There were thousands of machine guns, rifles, and tons of ammunition. They took the four trucks to a place near Alexandria
and placed them in the deep caves nearby for storage. They
went back to pick up the remainder of the weapons and they
saw Italians being loaded on British trucks that would take
them to prisoner-of-war camps. As they were unloading another truck in the caves at Alexandria, Abram had no inkling of
how important these weapons would become later on in his
life. Large signs were placed in front of the caves saying,
MINES — KEEP OUT. One could hardly see the weapons from
the outside anyway.

After having lost a large part of his commando in the Italian
bombardment and seeing the misery of thousands of the surrendering Italian soldiers, Abram suddenly felt older. It was as
if he were a robot, devoid of any feelings. He became the ultimate sergeant — cold, dedicated only to following his orders
no matter what the cost.

While driving through Mersa-Matruh with their second
load of weapons, they saw Captain Keymer waiting for them at
the military police checkpost. Abram asked him how he got
there. Keymer said, "It's much easier to hitchhike here in the
desert than in London." He told Abram that he had made
arrangements for the remainder of the unit to stay in the barracks of the Egyptian army close to Mersa-Matruh and to wait
for reinforcements. The barracks had sustained quite a bit of

damage during the fighting with part of the roof missing and most of the windows and doors broken. The commandos were unphased. They had water, sinks, and latrines. In the barracks nearby were Australians and Indian Sikhs; they were in good company. For a while, it seemed as if they were on a vacation. Eight days later reinforcements arrived. Sergeant Levin, a Jew, came with thirty men to replace their losses. He was very tall and blond. He looked like a typical Englishman, and was usually mistaken for one until he started to talk.

They continued their training without much pressure. The whitewashed walls of the barracks that survived the shelling inspired Abram's artistic creativity. Using soft pencils and pastels, he started to draw life-size, scantily dressed pin-up girls on the walls. In no time he became famous in the camp. The demand for his creations was unbelievable. He had to work overtime to fill the requests. The Australians especially were going crazy, bringing him boxes of beer and cigarettes in payment for a wall painting. It was funny to see the reaction of these men. Abram would never forget the face of a big, overweight corporal who came to see him late one evening. With tears in his eyes, he said, "Sergeant, what did you do to me? I can't sleep anymore." A group of senior officers came to check out his creations after a Sergeant Major complained about the introduction of "pornography" to the camp. They quickly decided that Abram's work was art. They congratulated him on his talent and encouraged him to continue with his painting.

In the meantime, the situation in North Africa had changed drastically. After the fall of Crete and Greece, heavy German bombers based in Creten airfields were hitting Alexandria and it's port around the clock. They were using "block busters," a bomb with a huge amount of explosives and a thin steel shell. Those bombs didn't penetrate the target, they exploded on the surface causing havoc to entire neighborhoods. The German air force controlled the skies, bombing ammunition depots and strafing camps.

Abram's commando was hastily called in to lend a hand in the construction of an underground ammunition tunnel, dug out in the rocky hill close to the base of Mersa-Matruh. South African mining engineers were directing the works. Abram and his men drilled holes in the rock and packed them with gelignite. After each explosion, they would load the carts with pieces of the rock and push them up hill. They went deeper into the rock wall every day. There was no ventilation, and after each explosion, the heavy fumes remained in the air, causing the men to cough. After four weeks, their lungs were in bad shape, and they could hardly keep up the pace. They were very happy to be relieved finally by an Australian unit. The South Africans were Boers, and were openly pro-German. Abram couldn't stand them. To him they were a bunch of arrogant Nazis.

The situation in the Western Desert was getting worse from day to day. General Alexander greatly weakened the English forces there when he transferred large numbers of troops to Greece. He did not anticipate the arrival of German units on the African front, which were dispatched to save the beaten Italian Army. It became obvious to the Germans that they could not rely on their Italian allies to hold off the British from capturing all of North Africa. The German High Command knew that by capturing Egypt and the Suez Canal they would be able to enter the Middle East, and from there, India. Conversely, if the British got control of North Africa, they could threaten Gibraltar and through it, western Europe. Until that time, there was only a small number of Germans with the Italian Army, mostly instructors and technicians. Now the German High Command decided to send General (later Field Marshall) Erwin Rommel with an expeditionary force to, in effect, take over the command of this war theater. Rommel had shown great leadership in the battles of Poland and France, and was considered to be one of the ablest, if not *the* ablest, general in the German Army.

Almost immediately after the arrival of his Africa Corps to

North Africa, Rommel demonstrated his great ability, as well as the superiority of the German weapons. He began his offensive at the end of March 1941. At the time, the British, having defeated the Italian army in December, 1940 and January 1941, occupied all of Cyrenaica including Benghasi. Rommel dealt a quick blow to the British units, recaptured Cyrenaica, surrounded Tobruk, which was a powerful British base, and drove on to Capuzzo (west of Solum). He was repulsed twice at Tobruk, but the British in turn suffered reverses when they tried twice to relieve the besieged garrison.

The Germans came well equipped for desert warfare. They brought with them tanks that easily out maneuvered their British counterparts, as well as mobile artillery. They introduced the excellent jerrycan for petrol and water. Even their dress and food suited the desert conditions. It was a total surprise to the Brits, and very worrisome as well.

The British were now losing battle after battle. Abram's commando, after a short recuperation from the arduous tunnel work, was given a very dangerous assignment. Sergeant Levin and Abram, each with eight men and a truck, were ordered to drive into a "no man's land" at night to bring back artillery ammunition that was left in the desert sands during a hasty retreat. The mission didn't look very promising, but they were trained well and were ready. Measuring the distance by time, they reached the described location without setting off any mines. For about an hour they walked around in the dark, poked sticks into the sand, but without any luck. Finally they gave up the fruitless search and returned to their artillery lines. The officers were furious. They needed the ammunition badly. The task seemed so simple to them and they felt they had been let down.

After a conference, it was decided that Abram's unit would go back at midday with a Corporal of the British Artillery Unit as a guide. After an hour or so of searching and circling, the Corporal, who was driving Abram's truck, found the ammunition. They started to load their trucks quickly; the drivers kept the engines running. They were very close to the German lines and they were spotted. They were in the middle of loading when a Stuka flew down toward them with its machine guns blazing. A minute later a second Stuka joined the first in the attack. The planes came down so low that Abram could actually see the pilots' smiling faces. Bullets were tearing up the ground. The strafing was furious and Abram was afraid that the Stukas had killed most of his men. The corporal, who was their guide, was shot through the head and chest; he was dead. Abram pulled his body up onto the seat. There were four other badly wounded men in Sergeant Levin's truck. Luckily the engines weren't hit and they drove off at full speed. They returned to their artillery positions. The officers were not happy because the commandos came back with a relatively small amount of ammunition. When they started shouting, Abram asked them to talk to their corporal, without mentioning that he was dead. When the officers looked into the truck, there was no more arguing.

A week later, they went back to *The Midway*. They received a very warm reception from old friends. There were noticeable changes: many more anti-aircraft guns were mounted; there was stricter discipline regarding lights. It was forbidden to light a cigarette on the deck. They were told that *The Midway* was now top priority on the German list of targets. Big balloons on steel cables, high in the sky, covered the entire zone of Alexandria harbor. There was a spirit of defiance in the air. Every night there was high-level bombing by the Germans. The sky was lit up by huge searchlights and anti-aircraft explosions. They had to stay under cover, not only because of falling bombs, but because falling fragments of anti-aircraft shells were dangerous as well.

Keymer called in the unit to give them a new assignment. They were to be taken by ship to a place behind German lines, land on shore in small wooden boats, hide until a German convoy appeared, and then to attack and destroy it. The commando consisted of forty-four men. They discussed the most effective way to accomplish the mission using, of course, the element of surprise. It was stressed that the most daring attack would produce the best results and be the safest. It was early May 1941. They were transferred to their old friend the *Voyager* and were welcomed aboard like good old pals. The frigate took them westward but stayed away from the shore.

It was nighttime. After the *Voyager* passed Tobruk, it turned south at full speed. Two miles from shore the ship circled and began floating. The commando descended into two boats. They were loaded with their Brens, lots of ammunition: grenades, a dozen or so mines, and two red kerosene lamps. The boats moved slowly, and the waves were strong. After reaching shore, they camouflaged the boats and climbed the almost vertical slope.

They formed four groups and went looking for the macadam road. They spotted two German trucks with their lights on. The trucks passed in front of them so they knew the exact location of the road. They advanced to positions about twenty meters from the road. Using their little shovels, they dug holes in the sand and placed the mines on the north side of the road. Nothing was moving. Suddenly they saw a line of lights on their right moving east towards Tobruk. The port of Tobruk was still in British hands, but it was besieged by the Germans. The Jewish 5 M.T. Transport was in Tobruk as well. As planned, they placed the two lit red lamps on the road. The lead truck stopped and so did the others. The Germans in the first truck jumped out of their truck and lit up their cigarettes. Some of them were urinating while talking about the meaning of the red lamps.

Forty-four Bren guns opened fire all at once. The commando started throwing hand grenades. The Germans, bewildered, tried to run because a number of their trucks were exploding, setting fire to the others; but those that did were killed by the Bren guns. Abram and his men were amazed to see such a complete destruction of the convoy. Not a single German managed to escape. The commando could not keep their eyes from the burning trucks which lit up the skies. They went down the slope, climbed into the wooden boats, and went back to the *Voyager*, which was signaling its position to them by discharging its guns. The unit sustained no casualties. That night, the captain of the *Voyager*, who had seen the flashes of explosions from far away, treated them to a barrel of rum.

In the meantime, Tobruk's siege was lifted and the besieged Jewish transport unit, the 5 M.T. became the 178th R.A.S.C. and was moved to Qena. A year and a half later Abram joined that unit as the Workshops Officer. Later in the war, after the British broke through the German forces at El Alamein in 1942, Abram brought his colleagues to the exact spot where his commando destroyed the German convoy. Parts of the burned trucks were still there.

The *Voyager* became Abram's base. It was a small ship, and when the sea got rough, many aboard became seasick. On one occasion, Abram was swept off by a strong wave. He was thrown into the air, and in the last second, was able to grab hold of a steel cable and held on to it for dear life.

They were moving up and down the Mediterranean, occasionally stopping at Alexandria for provisions and war matériel. The *Voyager* was bombed several times. The ship's two pom-pom guns kept the German planes from strafing them. Luckily the high-level bombings weren't too accurate and only a couple of bombs fell into the sea close enough to the ship to cause a small amount of damage. The ship's welders were kept busy repairing the holes. Army intelligence informed them that, for the moment, the Germans ceased to run truck convoys at night along the coastal road. Apparently, the destruction of the convoy by Abram's men had made them more cautious.

It was decided that, for the time being, they would direct their efforts to laying mines. Within three weeks they made four landings on the coastal road. They were able to place their mines in at least seven places between Sidi Barani and Derna without being detected. During one mission they pushed an abandoned, damaged truck into the middle of the road, and placed their mines at the side of the road where anyone trying to bypass the truck would be blown up by the mines. Just for fun, Abram, using a piece of chalk, drew the picture of the Jewish star, the Mogen David, on the mines. He was trying to recruit the help of God himself.

Since the mine laying missions took place at night, they used the moon to help them determine their location. They felt relatively safe at night in the desert. After a while they became more and more confident of themselves. Abram doesn't remember ever being scared during the missions. Once, after having landed behind German lines, the unit was very close to the road and saw two enemy tanks, one towing the other with a chain. The tanks were stopping from time to time because of engine trouble. The commando heard shouting, "*Hans, die kette.*" (Hans, the chain). The commando let the tanks pass as they had no effective weapons against them.

After a few weeks, they stopped the mine laying and went back to blowing up enemy water pipelines. Loaded with bundles of gun cotton, primers, detonators, and very long fuses, they reached the pipelines close to Bardia. They packed the pipes with explosives in several places. In order to magnify German casualties, they would place mines on both sides of the road, light the long fuses, and then run at top speed. They could hear the explosions shaking the ground. The Germans had to repair the damaged pipelines promptly because water in the desert was precious.

Those were happy days for Abram. He felt good. He was accomplishing something. He was killing Germans and helping the war effort. He was counting the hours between missions, anxious to go on another one. In Poland he was frustrated; here he had the weapons and could fight his enemies. He was walking tall.

New information came in regarding enemy convoys. The Germans apparently resumed their around-the-clock transports. Abram and his men started to prepare for a new attack. This time the *Voyager* let them off east of Tobruk where the heaviest enemy traffic was observed. After they camouflaged their boats, they came to a slope that was not too steep. They wandered around a bit looking for a suitable spot for the attack. This time they did not use the red lamps.

The macadam road was damaged by bombs and shelling in many places. They laid the mines along the road for maximum damage. They needed to slow down the convoy. They dug in the sand and waited. Nothing happened for a long time, and some of the men even fell asleep. Then the trucks came but it was not a very big convoy. From their positions in the darkness, they couldn't tell what kind of vehicles were in the convoy. The vehicles slowed down because of the damaged road. The commando opened fire all at once and then something unexpected happened. Suddenly, from the front, rear, and center of the convoy, armored trucks came out heading directly toward them, blazing away with heavy machine guns. There were no mines on their side of the road to stop them.

They threw hand grenades at the armored trucks and started running. Keymer shouted. "To the sea, and swim! Stay away from the boats, swim!" The boats were too far to their right, anyway. The armored trucks, firing nonstop, tried to encircle them. The Germans had no trouble in descending the relatively mild slope and came down in pursuit of Abram and his men shooting at them.

Abram ran down the slope rolling and falling several times. When he reached the sea, he dropped his gun, his belt with the pouches, pistol and knife, and with bullets whistling all around him, began to swim. He realized that he still had his boots on, but it was too late. He didn't have a knife to cut the laces. He swam fully dressed realizing that this might well be the end of his life. He was alone in the cold November sea. He saw no one around him. Because of the darkness and the waves, it was impossible to see or hear anyone. He kept on swimming but was making little progress. He lost all sense of direction. Because the waves were filling his mouth with seawater, he had to keep his head high. His uniform and boots were very heavy, and he had to float often to get some rest.

After what seemed to be an eternity, Abram suddenly spotted a distant flash of light. With tremendous effort, he managed to get rid of his battle shirt. His hope renewed, he started to swim energetically towards the point of the flash. All he wished for now was that the ship would remain stationary. He swam frantically but was getting very tired. Then he saw another flash, this time closer to him. He kept swimming in that direction, but was completely exhausted, and was again losing hope. His thoughts were racing frantically in his head. He was ready to give up; he just couldn't move his arms.

Abram has no idea how long he stayed in the sea. It seemed forever. Suddenly, he saw an image of his mother standing at the table making pastry and crying. He said to himself, "You can't do it to her; just keep going." Re-energized, with his muscles practically frozen, he kept moving ahead. Suddenly he heard a whistle; they had spotted him. He was very close to the ship. He saw a man holding a long hook on the bottom step of the ladder. Abram grabbed it with his last drop of strength. They pulled him out of the water and then two men dragged him up the steps. He was unable to walk or even stand up. They carried him down to the engine room, stripped him of the remaining clothes and boots, and started massaging him. He was shivering so hard that he was unable to say a word. They gave him a small glass of rum. He drank it and passed out.

When he regained consciousness, he found himself laying

on a bench. He was the third man to be fished out of the sea. Subsequently, ten more were rescued. Thirteen men out of forty survived the raid. They never found the other twenty-seven members of the commando. They were all killed on the shore of the Mediterranean or had drowned in its dark waters.

Abram was unable to walk for an entire week. All the survivors were exhausted. Keymer had been the first one to reach the ship. The ultimate athlete, he could always outswim or outrun any one of them. Abram will always remember Keymer. There was a time during one of the training sessions when, after a 50 kilometer march in the desert, Keymer turned to him and said, "Silver," (that's how Abram was called) "take command." Then he ran far ahead of his unit in order to prepare hot water for his men. After their arrival at the base, he called for a quick inspection, patiently examining every sore foot for blisters. Keymer was the ablest and finest infantry officer Abram had ever met during his army career. Abram was proud when he overheard Keymer say to another officer, "I am not going into action without Sergeant Silver; the bastard is very resourceful."

*A note regarding The *Midway:* Abram remembers one day, as a brand new Captain, after the breakthrough at El Alamein he was pushing forward past Tobruk, and the convoy of his 178th R.A.S.C. was loaded with petrol and ammunition. They were all in a state of euphoria. Someone came up to Abram and told him he had heard on the German radio station that The *Midway* had been sunk in the Port of Alexandria. It was a very sad day for Abram. The *Midway* officers and crew were the finest of the fine, and it was Abram's good luck to get to know them well. The ship was sunk, but its mission was accomplished. The submarines of The *Midway* managed to sink every single German, Italian, or French tanker loaded with gasoline trying to reach the port of Tobruk before the great battle of El Alamein. Rommel had to retreat because he was left without petrol. The *Midway* sailors were the few that did so much for so many.

~ 7 ~

THE COURT MARTIAL

Abram and his men were in a dark mood as they discussed their situation. It was clear that, having lost the element of surprise, they could not continue to operate effectively behind German lines. A week later they got off the frigate at Solum, which was still in British hands. Knowing that there was virtually no chance, they were still hoping to find a few more survivors, but to no avail.

One day, news came about receiving reinforcements. The H.Q. of the 51st M.E. commando, including officers and staff, were arriving in big flat barges called X boats. They came from Alexandria, and were loaded with ammunition, petrol, and food supplies. Now they felt more hopeful; perhaps things were not as bad as it seemed.

One of the newcomers was R.S.M. McGee. Abram and McGee took an instant dislike to each other. Abram was highly regarded and received special treatment from many of his superiors. McGee was an outspoken anti-Semite and Abram did not like that. He was an uneducated Irish Catholic, who kept telling his fellow soldiers that the British were fighting the wrong war. His opinion was that they should fight the anti-Christ Russians and Jews instead of the Germans. Abram hated McGee with every fiber of his body. There were German Jews in the commando who had arrived in Palestine just a very short time before enlisting in the British Army. They spoke only German. McGee always called them "fifth columnists." Actually no one, including the officers, liked him.

It was decided that the entire commando would move up and settle, temporarily, in the comfortable caves of Solum. There were already rumors of sending the unit to Eritrea in East Africa. At one point during exercises, Abram and other men from his unit were climbing a cliff, carrying heavy boxes. Abram was close to McGee when one of his men slipped, dropping a box on McGee's foot. McGee couldn't restrain himself. He shouted, "You bloody fucking Jews." Abram saw red. He forgot where he was; he didn't think of the consequences of striking a member of his unit at a place close to the German lines. He hit McGee's head with the butt of his pistol. McGee fainted and fell down the slope. When McGee opened his eyes, Abram said to him, "Next time, it will be a bullet." McGee answered, "I will teach you a lesson you will never forget." He could see that Abram was seething and said nothing further.

After the mission was completed, McGee told Keymer about the incident. Keymer was close to Abram, but he apparently had no choice. He said, "You know how much I like you, but I cannot help you in this situation." He had Abram arrested and held in a cave. The whole unit was on Abram's side. That day there was a distribution of chocolates and a number of the soldiers threw the chocolates into the cave where Abram was held. They were expressing their feelings openly, and the English officers were concerned about the morale of the unit. Abram knew he was in deep trouble, but wasn't sorry at all for what he had done. He was thinking of the possible consequences. After all, the charge was extremely serious. He could get at least three to four years in an army jail.

A sergeant appeared in front of the cave. He let Abram out and escorted him to a ship which was bound for Alexandria. Abram was put in a cabin together with two Italian colonels who were prisoners of war, and a guard was posted in front of the door. When Abram entered, the two Italians sprang to attention. Abram laughed and told them, "Don't worry. I am a prisoner too, probably worse off than you are." Upon landing in Alexandria, another British Army sergeant was waiting for him. He escorted Abram to Camp Amaria, an army base twenty-five miles south of Alexandria. He said, "You will be held here until your court martial takes place."

Abram was under arrest in Amaria for about a week. During that time he was guarded by a British army sergeant. Then he was told, "Tomorrow your court martial will begin." He made sure that his uniform was clean and his army boots were well polished. The following morning he was taken out of his confinement and marched to another barracks.

He was brought into a room where he saw three British army majors sitting behind a table. The judges were Englishmen in their late thirties and early forties. McGee was standing to the side. The judge seated in the center, asked McGee to tell the court his version of what had happened. After McGee had finished, the judge turned to Abram and said, "Is what R.S.M. McGee said true?" Abram replied, "It is the truth, but not the entire truth." In his statement McGee said that he shouted at Corporal Amos, but he denied making the anti-Semitic remark. Abram told the judges that McGee definitely called Amos, "You fucking bloody Jew," otherwise he would have had no reason for hitting him. Abram said, "I'm a Jew from Palestine. There is no conscription in Palestine, and I volunteered to join the British Army so I could fight the Nazis. McGee is a Nazi in a British uniform. He was constantly telling the other soldiers that we are fighting the wrong war. We should be fighting the Jews and the Communists, not the

Germans." Abram told the judges that the act of hitting McGee was a result of an accumulation of his resentments towards McGee and it was triggered by McGee calling Amos, "You fucking bloody Jew."

The judges asked Abram several questions about his activities in the commando, the length of his service, etc. He was then told to leave the room and wait outside. He waited about forty minutes, still guarded by the sergeant. He was called back before the judges. The presiding judge told him the case was being dismissed and that he would be transferred to another unit. McGee listened to the verdict, his face impassive.

The sergeant took Abram to the Base Office where a letter of transfer was handed to him. In the letter were instructions commanding him to report to a British army base at Sarafand. He was told to get on a train destined for Palestine. After eighteen hours on the train, he came to Rehovot which was close to the Sarafand base. News about Abram's court martial travelled fast, and Jewish soldiers at the base gave him a hero's welcome. It was known that he was the first Jew in Palestine to volunteer in the British Army, and the distinction of being acquitted by a British Court Martial added a great deal to his prestige and popularity.

The outlook for Palestinian Jews was very grim at the time. Rommel was at the gates of Egypt and seemed invincible. A succession of Britain's best generals was unable to achieve a major victory over the "Desert Fox." Even Churchill acknowledged in Parliament Rommel's outstanding abilities (or was it, perhaps, an excuse for the British defeats). There was fear that one more major German victory would cause a collapse of the British defenses in Egypt and open, for the victorious Germans, the gates to Palestine, the entire Middle East, and eventually India, the crown jewel of the British Empire. There was a great deal of fear among the Palestine Jews. Thousands were volunteering to fight the Nazis and defend their homeland. About 5,000 Jewish volunteers were being trained by the British, most of them in the Sarafand base. There was no great love lost between the Jews and the English. The Jews resented the recent White Paper which severely limited Jewish immigration, prohibited Jews from buying land, and generally nullified the promises of the Balfour Declaration. But there was practically no other option, so young Jews were joining the British Army. The English officers did not fully trust the Jews, and the feeling was fully reciprocated. It was a marriage of convenience at best.

British officers were in charge of training the Jewish volunteers. Abram, with his experience, was made an instructor. He taught them how to use weapons, military tactics, how to survive in battle. There were about seventy men under his command, and on every Saturday there was a military parade called "Pass Out."

Six weeks later, after a parade, he got leave for the rest of the weekend. Just as he was ready to dismiss his platoon and leave for Tel Aviv, Abram sensed that there was someone standing behind him. He turned around and recognized Colonel Lester, the Commanding Officer of the entire Sarafand base. Abram called his platoon to attention, saluted, and said, "Ready for inspection, Sir." Colonel Lester said, "Carry on Sergeant. What's your name?" Abram said his name. The Colonel wrote down the name and asked him if he was British. Abram told him that he was from Palestine. Abram wondered what this was all about. Colonel Lester was considered, at the time, to be the most important British officer in all of Palestine. Did he spot something wrong with the way Abram handled his platoon? He had no way to find out, and he went to Tel Aviv to see his family. Clara was there, as well as Doctor Mattes and the others. They all heard about Abram's exploits and, naturally, were very proud of him.

This was early in 1942, and there were rumors about German atrocities, but no reliable information about the mass murder of Jews that began in the late summer and fall of 1941 in Ukraine, Belorussia and, on a more massive scale, in Poland in the summer of 1942. As far as the fortunes of war were concerned, the British were being beaten by the Germans everywhere. First, of course, was the debacle in France in 1940, then defeats in Africa in 1941. Bad news came also from the east where the Japanese launched a surprise attack on Pearl Harbor on December 7, 1941, and destroyed a large part of the U.S. Pacific fleet. In quick order, they overwhelmed General MacArthur's forces in the Philippines and landed on the Malaysian peninsula.

The British didn't fare any better elsewhere. The Singapore fortress surrendered to the Japanese on February 15, 1942. This was a truly disastrous loss for the British Empire. The British General Percival went out with a white flag and surrendered to the Japanese General Yamashita the fortress together with close to 80,000 troops of the British Empire, mainly British, Australian, and Indian, with some local Malayan and Chinese units. Singapore had been considered the strongest fortress in the world and was synonymous with the power and prestige of the great British Empire. The future looked very dark for the British and indeed for the entire free world.

There was some good news, however, that brought new hope to the beleaguered Jews in Palestine, and indeed, to the rest of the Allies. First, after Pearl Harbor, America was finally in the war. Everyone believed that, in time, the colossal American industrial machine would gear up for huge production of all kinds of weapons and other war matériel. Second, there was good news from the Russian-German front. In the initial assault, the German war machine overwhelmed the surprised defenders, destroyed the Soviet armies in its path, took millions of prisoners, and advanced deeply into the enemy territory. All of Ukraine was in German hands with its largest industrial complex in all of the Soviet Union (and the Ukraine was considered the bread basket of the Soviet as well). German troops surrounded Leningrad and they were approaching Moscow. The German advance patrols could see the Kremlin's basilicas through their field glasses. Then the miracle happened, some-what similar to the one that destroyed Napoleon's armies in 1812. "General Winter" came to Russia's rescue. First the roads became so muddy that the German military vehicles could hardly move. The temperature fell well below 0°F and the German soldiers were completely unprepared for it. Hitler was so sure that the Russian campaign would be over before the onset of the winter of 1941–1942, that he didn't provide any warm clothing for his troops. (On October 3, 1941, he announced in the Berlin Reichstag, "The Soviets are defeated and only mop-up operations remain.") Now German soldiers were freezing to death by the thousands. Tens of thousands lost their feet and hands to frostbite and were packing the trains heading west for hospitals. The Soviets regrouped, brought in fresh divisions from Siberia, and under the leadership of Marshall Gregori Zhukow, dealt the Germans their first major defeat of World War II.

The Russian soldiers suddenly felt that the Germans were not a superior race after all. They were human; they could be beaten. The Russians knew that they had no choice. It was beat the Germans or perish. They knew now the Germans were killing civilians by the hundreds of thousands. They knew of prisoner-of-war camps where the Germans gave their Russian prisoners no food at all and let them starve to death.

Conversely, the Germans suddenly found out that the *Untermenschen* (subhumans) could fight, and indeed, beat them by using modern weapons of warfare. A great fear entered the German hearts. Maybe Hitler was wrong, maybe it was a mistake to attack the Soviet Colossus. From the winter of 1941–1942 on, to be sent to the Russian front was the one thing that Germans soldiers feared the most.

$\sim 8 \sim$

A BRITISH ARMY OFFICER

But the good news from the Russian front did not change the situation in Palestine. The Russians were far away, but Rommel and his Afrika Korps were close, threatening the very existence of Palestine Jews. Not only were they afraid of what the Germans might do to them, but also of Arabs who would be free to kill Jews under the German occupation.

Thousands of Jewish volunteers in Palestine were organized into units, trained mostly by British officers and a few Jews like Abram, who had gained experience fighting the Germans in Africa.

Abram returned to his barracks late on a Sunday evening. Pinned to his bed pillow was a British Army envelope in which he found an order to report to the Officers Cadres School on Monday morning. Abram thought that he would be giving the future British Army officers their basic training. Early on Monday morning Abram polished his boots so well that he could see the reflection of his face in them. He wanted to make a good impression on the young officers-trainees.

After his arrival, he reported to Captain Laizel. To Abram's surprise, Captain Laizel informed him that he, Abram himself, would be trained to become an officer of the British Army. Abram was truly stunned. If he successfully completed the course, he would become a Second Lieutenant in his Majesty's Army. The officer training unit consisted of 120 men, all Jews except for three Palestinian Arabs and two Maltese.

Apparently the British commanders, having to absorb thousands of Jewish volunteers into their army, decided to create all Jewish units as part of the British Army instead of integrating the Jews into all British units. To make sure that they had full control over these new formations, they assigned practically all British officers to command them. They wanted to have a small number of Jewish officers as well, but the top positions were assigned to regular British Army officers.

Many of the Jewish trainees were Haganah members recommended by the Jewish Agency. Moshe Dayan, who later served as Chief of Staff of the Israeli Army, and Yitzhak Rabin, the future Israeli Army leaders, were too young at the time to serve. A number of former Wingate trainees, including Laskow, Prihar, Akavia were all in the training program.

The course was exceptionally tough. There was constant training in rough terrain, obstacle courses, weapons, and special missions. It was too difficult for a great majority of the trainees. After four months the training program was finished, and those who passed it celebrated, only 11 men of the 120 successfully completed it. Eight were Jewish, including Abram, two were Arab and one was a Maltese Englishman. One of the Arabs, by the name of Valid Madani, served later in the 1948 War of Independence as Brigadier of the Arab Liberation Army under the political leadership of Shishakly. After this army was smashed, he fled to Kuwait. He and Abram were on very friendly terms when they were in France. At that time he said to Abram, "In the future, we will have to fight on opposite sides, but we will always remain friends."

Captain Laizel came into Abram's barracks and said to him, "Tell me, what makes you Jews better than the English? You completed the program in less than six months. It takes a full year to train an English officer." The new officers received a discharge from the regular army and were given the King's Officer Commissions. The trainees who failed to make the grade were sent back to their units as sergeants or ranks below that.

The Officer-in-Charge knew from Abram's biography sheet that he was a trained car mechanic. The British were very short of good mechanics, so Abram received orders to go to the Sarafand workshops so that they could check him out and make sure that he really knew his stuff. After two weeks, Abram came back with a letter full of praise. It stated that during the two weeks, Abram was successful in completely overhauling automobile and truck engines and transmissions. The Officer-in-Charge was very happy to read the letter.

Shortly after, Abram and Gubernick received orders to join the 178th Unit of the Royal Transport Service. This was an overwhelmingly Jewish unit of about 700 men. It included a small number of English sergeants, and was stationed at Quena, Egypt, near the Sudanese border. Abram was placed in charge of the workshops, and was told that if he did his job well, he would be made Captain in two years.

Abram, as well as most of the other members of the 178th unit, believed that the British would be unable to hold Egypt and that they were preparing to leave. It was the beginning of June 1942, and the 178th, among others, was engaged in building a road to Safaga, a port on the Red Sea. This fueled the speculation that the British needed this road to evacuate their armies from Egypt. Certainly their record of fighting General Edwin Rommel, the Dessert Fox, was not encouraging. Letters from friends and relatives in Israel told of near panic, and that didn't help the troops' morale either.

The Egyptians, sensing that Great Britain was in trouble, began to show hostility to the British Army soldiers. They threw stones at them, and in one instance, actually stoned an English soldier to death. Anti-British signs were everywhere. To counteract this unrest, the British staged a military parade involving several thousand of their soldiers, hoping that this show of force would serve to calm the situation. Many new Jewish volunteer soldiers were sent to Egypt from Palestine, and their number reached 4,000. A Jewish Womens' Auxiliary Service was formed. It was attached to the British Army. Altogether there were now four Jewish units in Egypt. Major Aaron, a British Jew, was the Commander of Abram's unit.

Top leaders of the Haganah came from Palestine to discuss the situation with the leaders of the Jewish units of the British Army. The discussions dealt primarily with the question on what to do in the event of the British withdrawal from Egypt. They all believed that, in such an event, the Arabs would attack the Palestine Jews even before the German Army's actual arrival to Palestine.

One June 21, Fortress Tobruk, which was surrounded by the Germans during the most recent retreat of the British Army, surrendered. This was another body blow to Great Britain. Even Winston Churchill found it difficult to explain to his countrymen why this most important British military base in North Africa fell with such relative ease.

General Klopper, the Commander of Tobruk, surrendered with 35,000 of his soldiers. Klopper and his men were considered by many to be an elite unit of the British Army. An enormous amount of stores and weapons fell into the German hands.

Rommel, now in hot pursuit of the retreating British, was helped greatly by the captured British supplies. According to General Bayrlin, the Chief of Staff of the Africa Corps, at this time, 80 percent of Rommel's transport consisted of captured British vehicles. But even with this great catch which provided Rommel with transport, fuel, and food to pursue the retreating British, when he and his soldiers arrived at the Egyptian frontier on June 23, he only had forty-four tanks ready for action. The rest, as well as other vehicles, needed repair and refueling.

He was still determined to pursue the beaten British, but ran into obstacles created by his own colleagues. Field Marshal Kesselring flew in from Sicily the day after Tobruk's fall to argue against any further advance into Egypt. General Bastico, the Commander of the Italian forces in Africa (nominally Rommel's superior even though his army did not play an important part in Rommel's victories), ordered his troops to halt. Kesselring claimed that he needed the Luftwaffe units, which were supporting Rommel's offensive, to help capture British-held Malta. Malta in British hands made it difficult to move German troops and supplies over the Mediterranean to Africa.

Rommel, a master strategist, knew that this was a great opportunity to deal the retreating and disorganized British a body blow which might cause them to withdraw from Egypt. He continued to press his case. He even jocularly invited Bastico to dine with him in Cairo. He went over Kesselring's head and appealed directly to Mussolini and Hitler for permission to keep his drive going. Hitler was ambivalent and did not provide Rommel with a clear answer, but Mussolini, worried about another embarrassment in the event the attack on Malta would fail, sent Rommel a wireless message, "Duce approves Panzer Armee intention to pursue the enemy into Egypt." A few days later, Mussolini flew to Derna. A white horse was brought in especially for this occasion to take Mussolini for a victorious entry into Cairo.

The British General Ritchie, thoroughly demoralized by Rommel's victories, decided not to defend the Egyptian frontier. His excuse was that he needed to gain time by giving up additional territory (as he telegraphed to Auchinlech). This, in spite of the fact, that he still had remaining three intact divisions and three times as many battle-ready tanks as Rommel. The shock of Tobruk's fall was, without doubt, too much for him. On June 25 General Auchinlech took over the direct command of the British forces from Ritchie, and decided to move his forces all the way back to El Alamein, 150 miles deep into

Egypt and half the distance to Cairo. This meant abandoning the fortified position at Mersa-Matruh.

Now that Rommel got the official blessing to push forward, his Africa Corps progressed 100 miles in twenty-four hours. When he reached the Mersa-Matruh fortified position, he expected the British to put up stiff resistance. Undaunted, even though he had only sixty tanks (including the ones that were repaired) against 160 British tanks in front of him, he decided to gamble on speed and surprise. With only 2,500 German infantry and 6,000 Italian soldiers (which he couldn't count on too heavily), he attacked the demoralized British at Mersa-Matruh on June 26. By midnight, his tanks and armored units broke through and were twelve miles behind British lines. Even though two-thirds of the British forces managed to escape, 6,000 were taken prisoner, larger than Rommel's entire attacking German unit, and another vast number of weapons and supplies fell into the German hands. By the next evening Rommel's Panzers stood only sixty miles from Alexandria. It appeared that Egypt was finally within his grasp.

However, having pursued the British for hundreds of miles in a matter of days and with little fuel left, the Africa Corps was not in a strong position to move forward, or even round up the scattered British soldiers and prevent them from reaching the new British defensive positions at El Alamein. The El Alamein defenses consisted of four fortified "boxes," the northern-most of which was on the Mediterranean coast and occupied by the First South African Division. Rommel's weakened forces attacked a "box" further south at Deil el Shei, ran into some resistance, and was unable to take it until the evening of July 1.

The news of German successes caused the British fleet to leave Alexandria and withdraw through the Suez Canal to the Red Sea. Had the Africa Corps been successful in reaching the Suez Canal quickly, a major portion of the entire British fleet would have been trapped. The British Admirals were taking no chances. The situation was grim. British officers ordered the files in their Cairo Headquarters to be burned. The burning papers created a great deal of smoke and the British soldiers called that day "the Ash Wednesday."

It appeared that Britain was in danger of losing the entire Middle East. On July 2 and 3 Rommel attempted to continue his drive, but his forces were now down to twenty-six tanks, and some British reinforcements began to arrive. A stalemate began that, except for minor battles, lasted till October 23, 1942, when General Bernard Montgomery, now in full charge and with a greatly reinforced Eighth Army, began his offensive.

Rommel was bitter. He was no longer in a position to finish his job and reap the fruits of his victories. He blamed all this, and probably correctly so, on the lack of vision and support from Hitler's High Command. He knew that a relatively small number of additional tanks, planes, and fuel would have made the difference. He knew that strategically his superiors made a bad call and that capturing the Middle East would have had a material effect on the outcome of the entire war.

~ 9 ~

STEALING WEAPONS
FROM THE BRITISH

The disastrous British defeats on the desert front reinforced the Haganah's determination to get as many weapons as possible into Palestine to be used in a last stand defense in the event of British withdrawal and German entry into Palestine. There were heated discussions between the Haganah leaders and the Jewish officers of the British-Jewish units in Egypt. A decision was made that in the event of British withdrawal from Egypt through the Red Sea, the Jewish units comprising 4,000 soldiers would not join the British Army. Instead they would use an old, secondary Turkish desert road to Jerusalem to defend Palestine.

This, of course, would have amounted to mutiny, but the men felt that no matter what the consequences, their foremost obligation was to attempt to save their people and their homes. Even if unable to hold Jerusalem and Tel Aviv, they were prepared to make their last stand at Haifa. The more unstable the British position became, the more urgent the need was for more weapons. At one meeting Abram told his colleagues that he knew of a very large cache of weapons hidden in salt caves near Alexandria. There were thousands of rifles, machine guns, and other weapons that the Italians had surrendered, which Abram and his men hid in the caves while serving in the Commando.

Abram's statement caused great excitement among the Jewish officers. By far, this would be the largest, immediate source of weapons for the Haganah. The question was how to get them out of the caves and into Palestine right under the noses of the British Army. One way to get access was to bribe the guards. One of the Haganah leaders, Tiber, went back to Palestine and returned with a suitcase full of gold. The gold consisted primarily of English gold coins. The case weighed about fifteen kilograms (33 pounds). They handed it to Abram and wished him good luck in this dangerous mission. A soldier stealing from the British Army would be subject to an immediate court martial and execution. This entire episode was described in a book written by Moshe Karu and published in Israel in May 1993.

They supplied Abram with three trucks and drivers. A Jewish sergeant in the British Army, Arie Miller, went along to help Abram. Arie came from a family that was one of the oldest and richest in Palestine and which, among others, owned large tracts of land in Rehovot. They travelled at night, using secondary roads, and hid out in the daytime. In three days, they arrived in Alexandria.

Alexandria was truly cosmopolitan. It looked like a European city, unlike Cairo that had a Middle-Eastern flavor. The population was a mixture mainly of French, Armenians, Greeks, Italians, English, and Egyptians. On Alexandria's streets one heard languages from all over the world. Thousands of military and civilians were causing traffic jams; the bars were full of soldiers, suspicious-looking characters, and prostitutes. French was the language most commonly used; many of the girls were Greek. There was a feeling of impending disaster with Rommel's troops less than a hundred miles away.

Abram had his drivers hide their three trucks in a large

park with many trees. He took a cab, by himself, to the area where the caves with the weapons were located. The caves were surrounded by a huge military camp housing a New Zealand division. At the entrance to the caves was a unit of this division that was guarding the weapons. Abram went back to the center of Alexandria and stopped at one of the hundreds of bars. He struck up a conversation with a Greek waitress. He told her that he was looking for an old army buddy from New Zealand and wanted to know which bars were mostly frequented by New Zealanders. The woman was very helpful and telephoned several of her girlfriends working in other bars. Finally, she came back with the information.

Abram took a cab to the bar. He was in luck. Sitting there with a drink was the New Zealand Army major who was in charge of the unit guarding the weapons. Abram remembers the major's name well, but now, more than fifty years later, he does not wish to reveal it. He solemnly promised the major that he would keep his name secret and feels, that even today, either the major or his family might be embarrassed by the events described here. Abram introduced himself to the New Zealander and ordered a double whiskey for them both. They started to chat. Abram was very frank. He told the major how worried he was about the fate awaiting the Palestinian Jews in the event of another German victory. The major was sympathetic. He nodded his head in agreement, "Yes, they would all be slaughtered." Abram ordered more drinks. They discussed the war; life in New Zealand; the Arab-Jewish struggle in Palestine; women — all sorts of subjects.

The next day Abram came back to the bar and again started drinking with the major. He was still hesitant to tell him about the purpose of his mission. He went back to the bar again on the third day, and by now, he felt that he could trust the man. He believed that even if the major refused to cooperate, that he would not betray Abram to the authorities. Abram now showed all his cards. He told the major what the mission was about and admitted that their meeting was not at all accidental. Very tense, Abram awaited the man's reaction. The New Zealander sat in silence for a few minutes and then said, "Abram, I am very sympathetic to you and your mission, but you are asking me for something I just cannot do." Abram argued that in the event of Egypt's evacuation, the British would not have enough time to take the weapons in the cave with them and that they would then fall into German hands. But that still did not change the major's mind.

Abram was heartbroken. He knew how important the weapons were to the Jews. He hated the thought of failing in his mission, but he was not ready to give up. He came back to the bar the following evening and the drinking started again. The major drank heavily; he apparently felt badly about not being able to help his new friend. Abram entertained him with his war stories. He told him how, when he and his unit were desperately looking for a boat to evacuate them to England, a bunch of French prostitutes came to the port at St. Malo and how they brought dresses for the soldiers and offered to hide them. The major had never tasted real battle and was fascinated by Abram's war adventures. When he heard about the courage of the St. Malo prostitutes, he burst out laughing. He kept laughing and laughing, hardly able to contain himself. He asked his fellow officers who were at the bar to come over and asked Abram to tell them the story. The major said laughingly to his friends, "Maybe, if Rommel breaks through again, the Fatmas (the Egyptian women) will come here and save us."

Abram was getting the feeling that perhaps there was hope. He sensed that the major had really gotten to like him. As night feel, the major suddenly said, "Abram, I want you to meet me at 11 o'clock in the morning at a restaurant." He gave Abram the address of the place, but offered no explanation as to why he wanted to have the meeting. Abram felt a wave of excitement in his heart. He went back to his people, still in hiding with their trucks. He told Arie that this, perhaps, was the break he was waiting and hoping for, but there was an outside chance that it was a trap. He knew that he had to take the risk. He told Arie, "If I am not back by 2:30 P.M., you can assume that I was arrested, and go back to Quena with the trucks."

It was a nervous night for Abram. He could hardly sleep. Next morning he went to the restaurant a little before 11 A.M. and from a distance saw the major sitting at the end table. Two sergeants of the New Zealand Army were seated across the table. Abram became apprehensive; maybe he had misjudged the man. An officer of the British Army would almost never sit at the same restaurant table with sergeants. Perhaps these were military policemen who were there to arrest him. Since the major still hadn't noticed him, Abram hesitated, but just for a few seconds. He knew in his heart that the major was a good person and that he could trust him. Anyway, it was too late to back out now. He approached the table. The major got up and introduced him to the two men. He said, "Abram, these are my friends. We grew up in the same village. I trust them. I told them about your mission and we made a decision to help you. My men will be at the gate of the camp waiting for you. They will help to load your trucks, otherwise it will take too much time." He picked up a Bible laying next to him on the table. "Here, put your hand on this Bible and swear that if you get caught, you will never mention my name. You will say that you and your men came alone, and took the weapons without anyone's help. Forget me; we never met. If I survive this war, I want to go back home and tend my sheep again."

A wave of excitement swelled in Abram's heart. He looked with admiration at this man who had come from halfway across the world, and at the risk of his life, was willing to help people he didn't even know. Later that night Abram and his men went to the camp gate. One of the sergeants and three soldiers were waiting (the soldiers, of course, didn't know what was going on) and helped them to load the trucks with about 2,000 weapons, including many light machine guns. After they finished loading, they started back toward their camp in Quena. Abram never saw or heard of the major again.

It was dark and they didn't know the roads well. At one point, they were stopped by a few Arabs who kept shouting, "Stop, stop." Abram didn't noticed that the bridge they were about to cross had partially collapsed. Had they not been warned by the Arabs, at least the lead truck would have fallen into the deep waters, and they would all have been in trouble. They found an Arab who knew the side roads and who agreed to show them the way to Quena.

When they arrived back at the base, Abram reported to Major Aron who had not been aware of the mission. He was very cooperative, but frightened to death. Aaron said, "This is very dangerous; where can we hide them?" Abram found a large number of empty oil barrels, and with help from a few friends, placed the weapons inside these barrels, covered them up, and rewelded the covers. Over the next several weeks, they sent the weapons piecemeal to Kibbutz Ruhama in the Palestine Negev. The Haganah men were ready with an underground hiding place.

A few years later during the War of Independence, the arms were dug out and used to fight the Arabs. Levitza (now Levi), a Jewish sergeant who was a Haganah leader in Jerusalem, was involved in the smuggling of the weapons and later wrote a book about it.

Major Wellesley Aron wrote a book *Wheels In The Storm* published by Roebuck Books in 1974. In the book he writes, on page 93, "We had no anti-tank rifles and no Tommy guns. I, therefore, proceeded to Cairo to obtain additional weapons and ammunition . . . in addition Captain A. Silberstein and Sergeant Arieh Miller went to Alexandria and managed, unofficially, to obtain three truckloads of Italian rifles and ammunition which they brought back to the unit after a five day trip."

Major Aron, for reasons that are his own, is not telling the full story. Why would they obtain these weapons "unofficially"?

This wasn't done in the British Army. Why did the trip take so long? It seems that he knew what was going on, but did not want to admit it because he was a British subject, and disclosing the full story could have had repercussions for him and his family.

Abram became an instant celebrity among the thousands of Jewish soldiers. Tiber, when he found out about the success of the mission, jumped for joy. He asked, "Well I guess the gold came in very handy. Who did you have to bribe?" Abram told him, "I didn't give it to anyone. I brought it back for you. I tried to give it to a New Zealand officer, but he refused to take anything. He told me, 'Just forget my name.'"

Winston Churchill, now desperate to find a commander who could finally defeat Rommel, decided to place General Montgomery in command of all British forces in Africa. Dozens of ships were now arriving with supplies, ammunition, and weapons. The mood of the demoralized British had suddenly improved. There was even talk about a forthcoming British offensive.

Abram's unit, the 178th, was split into two smaller units (178th and 179th). They were ordered to move to Suez, then further up to the Genifa base north of Suez. One day the unit was sent with loads of ammunition and petrol to Amaria near Alexandria. Most of the tanks in the British Army could only travel thirty miles without additional oil supplies, so there was a constant need for the precious fuel. Near El Alamein, they saw a huge sign, "Remember, the only good German is a dead German." Monty (as General Montgomery was called by his troops) appealed to the soldiers' patriotism to do their utmost for their country.

The artwork on the left was drawn by Abram to
accompany the montage of photos of his graduation class
from the Hrubieszow gymnazjum in 1934.

On the beach in Tel Aviv
(*left*), 1934.

Abram (*right*) as a contruction foreman in Tel Aviv, 1935.

Abram's mother and older
brother, Moniek, before the war.

Pre-war: Abram's father (*left*)
with his friend, Roytman.

Abram's father, Fishel (*third from left*), with other
delgates of "Keren Haysod" of Poland.

Abram's parents and his grandfather, Noah (*center*).

Some of the British officer-trainees in Palestine, January 1942.
Out of 120 candidates, only eight graduated.

Abram (*right*) and Gobernik (*left*) in Palestine immediately after graduating from the British Army Officers' School.

As a member of Wingate's group, 1939.

Getting ready to repulse German invaders, England, 1940.

On parade (*Abram above* X) in London
before leaving for the mid-East, 1940.

A Russian bringing
supplies to the British
soldiers during the
El Alamein offensive
in November 1942.

Jewish casualties of the
"Suicide Commando" in
North Africa, 1942.

Abram (*right*) in
Innsbruck, Austria,
checking lists of survivors
while looking for Hy.

Portrait taken in Florence, Italy, 1943.

Abram lecturing on the effectiveness of cross-fire to the
Officer Cadres Corps in Palestine, Januay 1942.

With Brigadier Benjamin (*left*) in Antwerp, 1945.

Belgium, 1945: Abram (*left*) and Hy (*right*) after he
brought Hy from the German camp.

Abram (*far left*) with fellow officers in Antwerp, Belgium in 1945.

Graves of Jewish casualties from the last days of the war
in the cemetery at Ravenna, Italy, 1945.

~ 10 ~

EL ALAMEIN

As of October 23, 1942, Hitler's armies had achieved, on virtually all fronts, their greatest penetrations of World War II. The German Empire had never before controlled so much territory, conquered so many peoples, won so many battles. Almost all of Europe was under its domination (Mussolini, by that time had shown so much weakness, that he was reduced to being Hitler's puppet). The French and British armies were destroyed in the west, the best of the British Empire forces were repeatedly beaten in North Africa, and even though the Soviet armies still held on, the Germans occupied the most productive industrial and agricultural regions of the Soviet Union.

In 1933 Hitler, who at that time didn't have the support of the majority of the German people, was able to seize control of the German government only by force and manipulation. But now the great majority of the German people hailed him as their savior and a conqueror of Germany's enemies. One could see only admiration, love, and respect in the faces of millions of Germans, in the streets and public squares of Berlin, Nuremberg, and other major cities. With raised fists and shining, glowing faces, they screamed, "Heil Hitler; Heil Hitler." On October

3, 1941, Hitler announced in the Berlin Reichstag, "The war against the Soviet Communists has been won, only a mopping-up operation is needed." Even some of Hitler's erstwhile foes and skeptics in Germany were grudgingly admitting they were wrong; maybe Hitler's Third Reich would last 1,000 years. The Fuhrer, himself, began to believe that his military genius was far superior to that of his famed generals — here he was, the former corporal, proving time and again how much smarter he was than his so-called military experts.

In the west the British, with only a shell of their once proud army remaining, were hanging on by their fingernails, knowing full well that by themselves they could never defeat their enemy. All their hopes were now resting on the Soviet Army somehow miraculously recovering from its defeats, and most importantly, on America eventually coming to their rescue.

It was one of the ironic twists of history that at this very moment with most of the Germans celebrating victory, and with most of their victims in dark despair, the most amazing turnaround in the history of warfare was at hand. In a matter of only a few short weeks, the situation would be so dramatically reversed that it would suddenly become clear it was Hitler who was losing the war, and an Allied victory was now only a matter of time.

Three critically important events took place to completely reverse the course of World War II. They were: the defeat of the German Army at Stalingrad; Montgomery's decisive victory over Rommel at El Alamein; and the landing of a large American force in North Africa. This last was not a military victory, but psychologically it was of great importance. To the beleaguered Russians, it meant that America was in the war on a large scale with prospects of soon relieving the pressure on the Soviet armies. To the British, it was even more important. They knew that without America's large scale involvement they could never defeat Hitler. Conversely, to the Germans it was their worst nightmare come true. Not only had the British beaten their best general, and the Soviets destroyed an entire German Army, but America, with its enormous industrial machine and ever-growing Army, was joining the battle against them.

On November 8, 1942, the American operation "Torch" went into action. With little resistance from the Vichy French, General Patton's troops landed at Fedala, north of Casablanca, and Safi, 140 miles south of Casablanca. Additional landings took place near Oran the night of November 7, and met with somewhat stiffer resistance, but that was overcome as well. The landing at Algiers ran smoother because the French commander, General Mast, decided to cooperate with the Allied forces (there were some British Navy ships involved in the operations). The French Admiral Darlan, who was in charge of French North Africa, was at first undecided, then agreed to cooperate and that was very helpful in executing "Torch" on schedule. Had Darlan not cooperated, and had he succeeded in persuading the North African French Army to resist, things would have been much more difficult for the Americans. There were close to 120,000 French troops in North Africa, and they could have become a big, although not an insurmountable, obstacle.

These landings affected the entire military situation in North Africa. A few days before the American landing in the west, Montgomery and his soldiers broke through the last German resistance line at El Alamein. Now Rommel's forces and his Italian helpers had to worry about their western flank as well, and the Africa Corps soldiers were losing what confidence they had left in achieving a victory in North Africa.

Most important of all, Hitler's armies suffered their greatest defeat of the entire war at Stalingrad. The German Army Group B, including the VIth Army under General Paulus, advanced deep into the heart of Russia, and at the end of August 1942, it reached Stalingrad on the Volga River. The control of the Volga was important since it served as a main strategic route connecting the Russian armies in the north with the south of

Russia. Simultaneously, another German force, Army Group A, was advancing rapidly into the Caucacus Mountains area with its critically important oil fields. In September and October the Army Group A advance was slowed down considerably because of the mountainous terrain and its stretched supply lines. Army Group B had run into stiff Russian resistance in Stalingrad. For weeks the Germans battled the heroic Russians for the city. Resistance was fierce, and the Germans were forced to advance slowly, with each building and factory becoming a fortress blocking their progress. At the end of October, the Germans had control of most of Stalingrad, but there were still nests of strong resistance. By now though, the soldiers of Paulus' VIth Army were exhausted, suffered great casualties, and their supply lines were thin and insecure. The German generals were concerned about their flanks with Hungarian troops protecting the northern one, the Romanians the southern. They knew that their allies were not very reliable, but they still believed that the Russians were too weak to conduct an offensive operation.

They had good reason to worry. The Russians brought in fresh divisions from Siberia to the Stalingrad front. Led by the brilliant General Georgi Zhukov, they started their offensive on November 19, 1942. The Russians struck north and south of Stalingrad and driving through the fields covered by snow, drove deep behind the German front. The 330,000 Germans in Stalingrad, exhausted and demoralized by severe cold weather and fierce Russian resistance, faced the possibility of being trapped. The Russians didn't give them much time, and by November 23, their two pincer movements met at Kalach, about fifty miles west of Stalingrad. Paulus and his soldiers were now surrounded and their only hope was to get out — and do it immediately — before the Russians poured in more troops to make their escape impossible.

The German High Command, realizing what was at stake, ordered Meinstein's XIth Army (part of the Army Group A in the Caucasus Mountains), now redesignated as Army Group D, to move north and attack the Russian troops surrounding Stalingrad and save their VIth Army. Meinstein's soldiers drove a deep wedge into the Russian lines, but were stopped about thirty miles short of their beleaguered brothers. The Russians counterattacked and drove Meinstein's army back to their original position.

The only hope remaining for Paulus and his soldiers was to break out towards the west, if necessary in small units, and thus save his forces from total annihilation. Paulus, joined by many other German military commanders, pleaded with Hitler for permission to break out, but he would not hear of it. To Hitler, surrender of an entire army would mean terrible humiliation and he wasn't able to face it. The thought of failing to conquer a Russian city bearing Stalin's name nearly drove him crazy. He raved and ranted at his generals, blaming them for the disaster. Paulus' pleas were becoming more desperate, but Hitler wouldn't yield. Hermann Goering promised Hitler that his Luftwaffe would be able to supply the VIth Army from the air, but wasn't able to deliver much of the needed supplies. The ring of iron squeezing the hundreds of thousands of German soldiers was getting tighter and tighter. Hitler now knew that Stalingrad could not hold, so he was pressing Paulus to fight to the last soldier. He even bestowed on him the rank of marshal, hoping that Paulus, aware that no German marshal in history had surrendered to an enemy, would die fighting. Even this ploy didn't work.

The Germans, having already lost tens of thousands of their men in Stalingrad, fought in the ruins of this city and finally surrendered on February 2, 1943. Over 150,000 Germans were taken prisoner and sent on a march deep into Russia to prisoner of war camps. Only a small number survived the war.

Hitler now had to face not only a loss of one of his best armies, but also a growing demoralization of his soldiers and generals. Most of them knew the war was lost, and fought only because of their sense of duty to their country, and fear of reprisals from Hitler's henchmen.

Churchill, impatient for a victory, was pressing Montgomery for an early start of the offensive in Africa, but Monty didn't yield to the pressure. He wanted to make sure that he had sufficient supplies to deal Rommel a decisive defeat. Ships were arriving loaded with tanks, artillery shells, and other supplies, and the morale of the British soldiers began to improve.

So it was October 23 at 9:45 P.M. with Hitler's armies controlling virtually all of Europe, and standing close to Cairo and the Suez Canal, when General Montgomery's great El Alamein offensive began. To start, more than a thousand British guns pounded enemy positions for three consecutive days. Following this barrage, an infantry assault was launched. Two hundred and thirty thousand British soldiers, supported by 1,440 tanks were thrown into battle. Even though Edwin Rommel was begging for reinforcements, the German High Command gave priority to the Russian front where Hitler was hoping to finish off the Soviet armies so that he could later concentrate on the western and African fronts. Rommel's Africa Corps at that time only had 27,000 soldiers and 260 tanks. True, there were his Italian allies, but their 53,000 soldiers were poorly trained and their 280 tanks were obsolete and virtually worthless. In the air the British also had a decisive advantage. In addition, many of the convoys sent to resupply the Africa Corps were being sunk by British bombers and submarines, so they suffered a chronic shortage of fuel and ammunition.

Initially the attacking forces made good progress, but soon the depth and density of German minefields caused many British casualties. The British advance was slowed down. The Germans, helped particularly by their anti-tank guns, were able to temporarily stop the VIIIth Army's advance. A couple of days of maneuvering by both sides followed, and on October 28,

Montgomery started a new offensive. This new thrust again got hung up in the German minefields.

But even though the attacking British forces were suffering the loss of four British tanks for every German one, the ratio was still deadly to Rommel. In a letter to his wife written on October 29, he said, "I haven't much hope left. At night I lie with my eyes open unable to sleep, for the load that is on my shoulders. In the day I am dead tired. What will happen if things go wrong here? That's the thought that torments me day and night. I see no way out if that happens."*

Another attack was launched by the British on November 2. By now, however, given the previous history of the British defeats by the Desert Fox, there was great anxiety in London. The top British commanders and Churchill himself began to wonder whether, perhaps, Monty's armies were stopped. This time, however, their worries quickly changed to jubilation. After two days of intensive fighting, the Germans had almost nothing left with which to fight. Rommel had thirty tanks,, the British had 600. It was no longer a contest. On November 4, the VIIth and Xth Armored Divisions broke through as did the motorized New Zealand Division. Monty now had a chance to trap and destroy the entire Africa Corps, but once the German commanders gave the order to retreat, the German troops moved quickly to avoid being captured. The British still had an opportunity to close the gap, but they cautiously halted their advance at night and let the bulk of the remains of the Panzer Armee slip out.

Still it was a complete rout. The VIIIth Army took 10,000 German and 20,000 Italian prisoners. On the night of November 7, Rommel withdrew from Mersa-Matruh, more than 100 miles west of El Alamein (where Abram and his commando were active before). On November 11, the British captured Ca-

*The Rommel Papers, page 312.

puzzo, 150 miles further west. The Germans were preparing to put up some resistance at Mersa Brega, 400 miles west of Capuzzo, but the VIIIth Army, after a few weeks of receiving new supplies and reinforcements, was preparing a new offensive. Hitler and Mussolini knew the Africa Corps was in deep trouble. They ordered Rommel to hold the line at all costs. He told them that he needed fifty Panzer IV tanks and fifty anti-tank guns to be able to hold the Mersa Brega line. But the Tunisian front, where the First American Army was pushing eastward, was now getting preference. Rommel, in desperation, decided to fly to Rastenburg in eastern Russia to see Hitler personally. He told Hitler that his advice was to evacuate all North Africa. Hitler flew into a rage (as he by then frequently did when faced with new defeats), and refused to listen to any arguments. He insisted that Mersa Brega be held at any cost. Rommel went to Rome to see Mussolini. He was more realistic and gave permission to withdraw to Buerat. On the night of December 12, Rommel slipped away. His beaten troops went 250 miles further west to Buerat.

Another month had passed before Montgomery was able to receive enough supplies to resume his drive. But Rommel, who could now see clearly that asking Hitler for permission to withdraw anywhere was a mistake, made up his mind not to fight at Buerat or even at Tripoli. He knew that his best chance was to take the remainder of his army all the way back to the Tunisian frontier and the Gabes bottleneck where he could put up a much more effective stand.

During the great El Alamein battle, the Jewish units, the 178th (where Abram was), the 179th, the 462nd, and the 11th water tank unit (these were the four Jewish transport units taking active part in this battle), were right in the midst of Monty's offensive. They were supplying ammunition to the British front lines where the fighting was raging. The first German tank Abram saw was right at the seesawing front line. A German soldier's body was hanging halfway over the turret. Abram and his fuel trucks were delivering their precious cargo all the way up to the front, with shells often exploding all around them. While all this was going on, an incident took place that is described in the book, *The Jewish Transport Unit, 178 R.A.S.C., J.B.G. In the Desert and Europe: 1939–1945,* written by Mr. Moshe Karu, Secretary of Kibbutz Yakum, page 89.

The Cinderella Tale

We were camping near Capuzzo, licking our wounds after a hellfire passage, when out of the blue sky, we were surprised and honored with an extraordinary visit. The Chief of Staff, Head of Supplies for the whole VIIIth Army, Brigadier Clover, accompanied by two majors, came to visit our area in person.

Immediately his attention was drawn to the large number of knocked-out British trucks spread out all over the area. He turned to our workshops officer, Silberstein, and asked him, "How are you going to cope with such a large number of disabled trucks needing repair?" The reply from our workshops officer was brief and immediate. "This area will be clean by tomorrow, Sir."

It was evident that the Brigadier was not convinced, and our officer's reply was taken as showing off. The three H.Q. officers began asking him about his technical background. Brigadier Clover left, shaking his head.

To our great surprise, next day at noon, Brigadier Clover turned up again, and what does he see — a completely clean area, all the trucks were out on operation. He turns to Silberstein saying,

"Well done, Captain!" "Sorry, Sir," says Silberstein, "I am only a second lieutenant." "From now on, you are Captain Silberstein," and with these words, he left together with his escort.

Next day, two D.R.s with a written order from G.H.Q. VIIIth Army called on our Company Office. Silberstein was promoted to Captain. With his new rank, Silberstein ordered the assembly of all the workshops personnel. Excitedly he said to us, "It is you that promoted me, ahead of time. I got it because of your outstanding devotion, hard work, and excellent craftsmanship. I thank you!"

Another miracle. A fairy tale, but a true one.

Once the German resistance broke, the British tanks moved fast, and it was critical to establish a continuous flow of fuel to be able to take advantage of the breakthrough. As Abram's troops drove west, they saw hundreds of German and British military vehicles burned out and thousands of bodies lying in the sand. Even though the Germans were retreating rapidly, there were still a few German and Italian fighter planes bombing the advancing British. At Benghazi one of these attacks occurred and Abram and his men spent the night in a trench.

In Benghazi they came across a few of the local Jews who gave them a warm reception. The soldiers helped the Jews to reopen their school. They passed El Agheila as well as Leptis Magna, an old Roman town. The ruins were so well preserved one would think the Romans had just left yesterday. The ancient market and the houses were still in very good condition.

Finally they reached Tripoli which was taken on January 23. The port was severely damaged and sown with mines, but crews worked feverishly to repair and clear it, and the harbor was opened on February 2. A week later two thousand tons a day were being handled and Tripoli became a major resupply port for the advancing VIIIth Army.

In Tripoli a very pleasant surprise was waiting. There was a fairly large Jewish community and the people gave Abram and his men a great welcome. They were greeted with flowers and many of them were invited to stay in Jewish homes. It was Pesach and Abram enjoyed being the honored guest at the traditional ceremony and dinner. It had been a long time since he had been able to enjoy real Jewish food.

Unexpectedly, Units 178 and 179 received orders to remain in Tripoli and overhaul a number of trucks that were needed to serve an Indian unit. The trucks were in very bad shape, but the orders were to repair them in just two days. They worked non-stop and met the deadline of April 28, 1943.

Another exciting and unexpected event took place while Abram and his men were in Tripoli. The great man himself, Winston Churchill, flew in from Cairo and stayed in Tripoli for two days. He was exhilarated, naturally, by the first major British victory of the war. There was a parade in his honor with two British divisions marching by, spearheaded by pipers of the 51st Highland Division. At Montgomery's headquarters, Churchill addressed two thousand officers and men. He said, "Yet nightly pitch our moving tent, A day's march nearer home." It was a great well-deserved victory for Churchill and his army, especially sweet because it came after a long period of fighting alone against Hitler.

On April 30 Abram and his units left Tripoli and were on the way to Malta where they were scheduled to meet another Palestinian-Jewish unit, the 462nd with its 700 men, who were coming by boat from Alexandria. Malta, at that time, was a sore in the German-Italian position. It was blocking their ship movements in the Mediterranean and was a base for the British Navy and Air Force. The Germans knew that they had to keep the pressure on Malta to prevent the British from resupplying their

VIIIth Army, and were constantly bombing the island as well as all the Allied ships in the area. They were also using submarines to try to stop the flow of matériel to the British. Unfortunately, one of the two ships carrying Abram's unit was hit by a torpedo on the way to Malta and sunk. One hundred forty-two Jewish soldiers perished in the Mediterranean waters. The others were rescued by another ship and brought back to Tripoli. The ship Abram was on was one of the first to break through the German blockade without sustaining any damage.

~ 11 ~

MALTA

Life was difficult for Abram's unit in Malta. The island was under continuous attack from German and Italian war planes based in Sicily, which was only sixty miles away. The German General Staff developed a detailed plan for invading Malta, and Hitler was pressing his generals to get going. Mussolini was hesitant because he was afraid that, if his forces proved to be inept again, he would lose whatever remaining respect Hitler had for him. It was, perhaps, Mussolini's trepidation that saved Malta because the British defenses were not very strong, and the proximity of the Axis air bases would have made it difficult for the Allied naval and air forces to offer significant support.

Because of the German bombardment, the Maltese population, which was primarily Italian, was spending a lot of time in catacombs. Housing was very scarce and Abram's unit was placed in a partially destroyed building. There was a small colony of lepers living in that building as well. A Doctor Cavallo was taking care of the lepers. He was a frequent visitor to Abram and his men, assuring them that they had nothing to fear from contagion. Most of the British troops lived in the fortifications. Close by was the airstrip with a small number of British planes. Abram became friendly with a few of the pilots.

Now let's go back a little bit in time and see what happened to the remainder of the Africa Corps. It was in Tunisia where the final chapter of the Axis defeat in North Africa was being played out. After the initial landing to the west, the inexperienced American troops suffered a defeat. Even though by now Rommel was a sick man, he was still showing his genius for warfare. He used good judgment by striking the American forces before Monty's pursuing VIIIth Army caught up with him. His famous and experienced 21st Panzer Division, sent back to Tunisia earlier, was now commanded by General Von Arnim. Together they attacked the American 2nd corps. Even though some American units managed to escape, the main body of the 2nd corps was surrounded and largely annihilated. Forty American tanks were lost. Rommel wanted to press his attack. He wrote, "The Americans had no battle experience, and it was up to us to instill them with a deep inferiority complex from the beginning."

But General Ziegler, who was in charge of the German attack, hesitated and this gave the Americans a chance to fall back to Lbeitla where they were able to put up a stiffer resistance. This delayed the German capture of Lbeitla, but they were successful in destroying or capturing 100 American tanks and taking 3,000 prisoners. Rommel was pressing for a continuation of the offensive while he had the Americans on the run, but General von Arnim was stalling again. This again gave the Yankee soldiers time to fall back to a new position. But even with this new delay, Rommel was able to capture the strategically important Katherine Pass. When it became apparent to Hitler that Rommel's actions were being hampered by a divided command, Hitler placed him in full command of all Axis forces in Tunisia on February 23.

The setback suffered by the Americans encouraged Hitler

to send new reinforcements to Tunisia, even though it was now clear that North Africa was lost and that he was just throwing the badly needed German reserves to the wolves. Hitler again showed his stupid stubbornness and unwillingness to retreat from any position. He did it in Stalingrad and now he was repeating the mistake in Tunisia. The self-proclaimed military genius was responsible for the death or capture of hundreds of thousands of the best German soldiers that were badly needed to beef up crumbling German defensive positions elsewhere.

After the American resistance had stiffened and a large number of reinforcements began to pour in, Rommel, who never lost his ability to think clearly, knew it was time to quit and save the bulk of his army in Africa. He returned to Europe and was pushing for an order to evacuate. He said, "It was plain suicide" to continue to fight in North Africa. All that was in vain. Hitler, annoyed by Rommel's suggestions, decided not to send him back to his beleaguered army. From this point on it was only a matter of a short time for the nutcracker to close. On May 13, 1943, the Axis forces, squeezed on all sides by the U.S. First Army and the British VIIIth Army, capitulated. About 170,000 were taken prisoner or killed; a few months after Stalingrad, where over 300,000 Germans were killed or taken prisoner. It was clear the Allies were winning the war. But Hitler knew that with all the atrocities he had committed, the end of the war would mean his death, and so he was determined to continue fighting. Deep down he was well aware that millions more of his countrymen would die as a result, and the Fatherland would be largely destroyed. It was one of these strange quirks of history when one man acting against all reason had the power to cause such incredible damage to the rest of the world.

In the meantime, Abram and Unit 178 were hard at work moving large amounts of supplies for the VIIIth Army, apparently getting ready for the invasion of Sicily. One day Edward VIII, the British king, flew in and a parade was given in his honor. In addition to the soldiers of the VIIIth Army, thousands of local people who were friendly toward England came out to take a look at the monarch. Even some monks were in the audience. Malta was the home of many monasteries, and thousands of monks were seen in the streets of the island.

One day in early summer, a British bomber pilot invited Abram to join him on a mission in his plane. He was planning to take aerial photos of parts of Sicily. Abram had never been in an airplane before and eagerly accepted the invitation. Right at the takeoff, the right wheel of the bomber burst. Ground control told the pilot to land the plane on its belly. The pilot disregarded the order and flew to Sicily. He thought he could land safely by balancing the weight of the plane on the remaining wheel. On top of the wheel problem, they had used more fuel than anticipated; it was running low. The pilot told Abram, "Pray to your God. I don't think mine would help."

They threw all the ammunition overboard before landing. The plane hit the ground hard. The engine caught fire, and the fumes made it difficult to breathe. There were three exits. The pilot, the co-pilot, and another man got out. Abram was next in line. He got his head and part of his torso through the hatch, but the remaining airman was trying to push himself out through the same hatch. Abram's torso and the airman's head got stuck in the hatch. Finally the airman started to choke and pulled his head back. Abram made it onto the wing and the others pulled him away from the burning plane. His legs and lower torso were badly burned. He spent the next two and a half months in a British military hospital.

The German Luftwaffe, though by now it had lost its numerical superiority, was still frequently bombing targets in Malta. While these attacks were taking place, the hospitalized were taken to the catacombs. Abram couldn't be moved because of the severity of the burns, particularly to his legs, so he was the only patient left in the hospital during the raids. The treatment for his burns was very painful because he was dipped in saltwater to help the healing. After he got out of the hospital, he had a slight limp for a year or so, but that didn't hamper his performance as a manager of the transport workshop.

In the meantime, the Allies fortunes of war were continuously improving. In Russia, Hitler was determined to start a new offensive in spite of the tremendous losses his armies sustained in Stalingrad and the Caucasus Mountains. He assigned his best remaining armies for his final offensive on the Russian front. At dawn on July 5, 1943, the German armies struck the Soviet positions on the Kursk Salient. A million German soldiers, supported by 3,000 tanks (nearly all of the German armor available) and 2,000 warplanes attacked the Salient from the north and south. Their armies were led by General Kluge on the northern front, and by General Meinstein on the southern one. This time the Russians fully anticipated the offensive and were ready for it. Their soldiers, supported by many thousands of tanks, artillery pieces, and planes were waiting for the Germans. The biggest tank battle in history took place. Thousands of tanks were on the move in open fields trying to outmaneuver and destroy their enemy. After a week or so the German offensive achieved some penetrations, but then it ran out of steam, and the Russians launched their counteroffensive.

On July 12 the Russians attacked in the northern sector. In three days they advanced thirty miles. They were within fifteen miles of Orel, which became the linchpin of the German front. The Germans put up a stiff but only temporary resistance, and had to give up this key city on August 5. By capturing Orel, the Russians removed any remaining threat to Moscow. On August 5 they also captured Bielgorod. Now the whole German front was breaking up, and the Russians were advancing rapidly. On August 23, they captured Kharkov, one of the largest Soviet cities and took 25,000 German prisoners. In September, the German retreat became a rout. On September 25 the Russians took Smolensk, and early in November recaptured the capital of Ukraine, Kiev. By the end of December the Russian front stretched from south of Leningrad to Zhitomir in the Ukraine, Dniepropietrowsk and to Khersen near the Black Sea. Thus the Russians had pushed the Germans back and retook more than half of the territory occupied by the enemy.

They showed that they were now capable of defeating the Germans in the summer as well as in the winter. This course of events put great fear in the German hearts. They knew that these "untermentchen" were now capable of handling the most modern weapons and of beating them time and time again. From that point of the war on, the one thing that the Germans feared the most was to be sent to the Russian front. They knew what they had done to the Russian people during the occupation, and were scared to death of what the Russians would do to them, their families, their homes. Hitler was forced to use the S.S. on the front lines to intimidate the regular German soldiers in order to secure their obedience.

Abram and his 178th unit continued their work on Malta when an interesting and amusing situation developed. While fighting in Sicily, the British captured a unit consisting of thirty Russians who were used by the Germans to build fortifications. Since the British couldn't understand them, they shipped the Russians to Malta where they knew many soldiers in Abram's unit could speak Russian. The Russians were happy to be in Allied hands, especially now that they were with people who could understand them. The Russians were very talented. They did a lot of singing and were dancing the hopak and other Russian dances. One of their officers, when told that Unit 178 was Jewish, came over and drew a Mogen David Star on the sole of his shoe to prove that he was Jewish too. Abram had many interesting conversations with the Russians about their homes and war experiences.

~ 12 ~

ITALY

Things were going well for the Allies on the Mediterranean front too. The American VIIth Army, led by General George Patton, landed in Sicily on July 10, 1943, while Montgomery's VIIIth Army was landing further east on this large Mediterranean island. After some stiff initial resistance, primarily by the S.S. Hermann Goering Division, a race began between Patton and Montgomery for the glory of reaching Messina, which was separated from the Italian mainland by only a narrow strip of water, first.

Patton had to cover twice the distance of Montgomery's troops, but he drove his men relentlessly, often being on the front line himself. So when Monty's troops entered Messina from the south on August 17, they were greeted by Patton's soldiers, their orchestra playing a military march, and gleeful cries of, "Where have you tourists been?"

This feat, accomplished by the American general against overwhelming odds, received a great deal of publicity in the American and British press, and Montgomery never quite forgave Patton for beating him to the punch. Fifty-five thousand German soldiers were captured and thousands more killed.

Now the Allies were moving quickly. On September 3, Montgomery's VIIIth Army troops landed in Reggio across the narrow Straight of Messina. On September 9, 1943, the operation "Avalanche" began. The U.S. Vth Army under General Clark landed at Salerno, Italy about 200 miles north of Palermo and Reggio. This amphibious operation was supported by an armada of naval vessels and bombers. In the following days this beachhead was extended, primarily on its southern perimeter. Also on September 9, the First Airborne Division landed at Taranto in southeastern Italy. By September 30 the fast advancing VIIIth Army reached the Salerno area while the Americans broke out of the Salerno beach and joined their British allies at Auletta.

Sometime in December 1943, Captain Silberstein and his unit received an order to embark on a ship docked in the port of Malta. They were being sent to Taranto. Shortly after their arrival in Taranto, Abram's unit was moved in quick succession to Bari, then to Termoli, and finally to Foggia, with its huge airport serving many American and a few British air units. There were quite a number of Jewish pilots serving in the air squadrons operating from Foggia. Abram became friendly with a few of them, having met them at the officers' messhall.

Abram was placed in charge of repair shops taking care of vehicles in his unit and other units. The vehicles were kept busy transporting military supplies to the front. The American Vth Army was attacking the Germans on the western part of the Italian front, and Montgomery's VIIIth Army was pressing them in the east. Many American movie stars and entertainers came to visit the troops, among them, John Garfield, the star of many motion pictures. Garfield took a liking to Abram and came to visit him often. Garfield, a Jew, was proud to see Abram and his unit from Palestine fighting Hitler as volunteers. The actor was always surrounded by beautiful women which was, of course, welcomed by Abram and his friends. Italian girls were anxious to befriend American soldiers. It wasn't just the food and all the goodies they were receiving. Italian people, who are very warmhearted, never took a liking to the rigid and boastful Germans and were happy to see the outgoing and friendly Americans take over.

This was the first time in the war that Abram had the opportunity and was in the mood to have fun, and he dated many young, beautiful Italian girls who liked the tall, handsome Palestinian, not only because he helped them and their families with food and other necessities of life, but also because he was charming, learned to speak their language well, and treated them with courtesy and respect.

One day Major Aron asked Abram to set up a place where he could invite some Jewish-American officer friends of his. Abram got hold of a villa, which was newly built by a well-known fascist. There was no furniture or electricity in it, so Abram brought in a generator from the airfield, brought in some furniture, and was able to report to Major Aron that the place was ready to receive his guests. They set up tables, brought in delicious food and drinks, and invited about forty officers from various services, all American Jews, for their first dinner.

Major Aron, who was an ardent Zionist, spoke first. He told his American colleagues about Palestine, about Zionism, about the excitement with which Jews were building their own place in the sun. To his and Abram's surprise, the response was cautious and lukewarm. One speaker after another proclaimed that they were Americans first and Jews next. They were interested in helping their Jewish brothers, but didn't want to get involved too much. It was clear that the majority of the officers were so worried about being accused of not being American enough that they drew a clear line on their interest in Palestine. Aron and Abram were shocked. There they were — one a British Jew from a distinguished family risking his standing and career to some extent because of his open, full hearted, and sometimes clandestine support of Zionism; the other, a Polish Jew volunteering for suicide missions to fight Hitler, getting such a timid response from their American brothers.

Unexpectedly, a tall officer stood up and startled everyone by his statement. He said, "I'm from Texas and I am not Jewish. I'm a writer and I came here because I was curious about this meeting. The American colleagues of mine are not telling the full truth. Jews are not really liked by many, if not most, Americans. There is a lot of anti-Semitism in the U.S. The fact is, most Americans don't want Jews in America. I'm advising the Jewish American officers here to open their eyes. Go to Palestine and build your own country."

It was amazing. Abram felt that the Jewish officers became suspicious that the whole thing was a set-up planned by him and Aron. The meeting broke wide open, everybody was shouting, expressing their opinions, and discussions went on late into the night. Abram didn't sleep well that night. It hurt him to see the American Army's Jewish officers lack of interest in what he and other Palestinian Jews were fighting so hard to accomplish.

New political developments took place in Italy that had an important effect on the course of the war. Benito Mussolini was a by-product of the tensions and frictions among the many layers of people that made up Italian society. The Italians, by and large, are a happy, loving, easygoing people, but apparently many of them felt that a certain amount of discipline was needed in their country, and they supported Mussolini in his rise to power. Mussolini had visions of building an Italian empire, but he was being continuously frustrated by his people's unwillingness to give their lives to help him conquer areas of Europe and Africa in his pursuit of rebuilding the old Roman Empire. He did some good things for Italy. Unemployment had gone down and one of his proudest accomplishments was to make the Italian trains run on time. He was very aware of the mistake his country made in World War I by joining Germany and Austria, and since he didn't fully trust Hitler anyway, he delayed choosing sides in World War II until the last moment.

Only after the collapse of the Western front in 1940, when it became clear that Hitler was about to occupy all of western Europe, did Mussolini decide to join Germany and attacked France on the Riviera. But even then the small French contingents guarding the French-Italian border held off the Italian Army for a while, and surrendered only after the capitulation of the entire French Army took place. Mussolini again had to suffer the sarcasm of his German partners and keep excusing the poor performance of his soldiers. Time and again he was humiliated by his North African armies' defeats by the British. The embarrassment was even greater when a relatively small Africa Corps, led by Rommel, dealt defeat after defeat to the same British troops.

He was gradually reduced to being Hitler's puppet, and lost whatever support he had among the Italian people. Now a time had come when he had to face the wrath of his countrymen who held him responsible for the disasters which had befallen Italy. He was a dictator, so he couldn't blame anyone else for what was happening. The Italians held him accountable for the defeats in Africa, Russia, the Balkans, and Sicily, and the unavoidable occupation of Italy by the Allied Armies. There was great unrest among the Italian military and political circles. Leading Italians knew that if Mussolini was allowed to hold power, it would bring additional suffering to their people.

General Ambronio, the Chief of the Italian General Staff, with the support of the Duke of Acquarone, who was close to the Italian king, proposed an immediate withdrawal from the Balkans. Mussolini refused, but was no longer capable of enforcing his orders. The king opened contacts with Marshal Badoglio, and together they devised a plan of how to get rid of Mussolini. Even elements of the Fascist Old Guard agreed to join others in summoning the Fascist Grand Council and confronting Il Duce with an ultimatum.

At 5 P.M. on July 24, the Grand Council met. The police co-operated and relieved Mussolini's personal bodyguards of duty. Mussolini addressed the Council and tried to convince its members that all was not lost, that this was a moment to tighten the screws, mobilize new forces, and continue to fight the Allies.

Apparently, Mussolini's speech had little effect on his listeners. Grandi introduced a resolution calling upon the king to assume more responsibility, in effect, ending Il Duce's dictatorship. Mussolini was shocked and embarrassed to see his own son-in-law, Count Ciano, voting against him. Mussolini's remaining supporters, seeing they were being outmaneuvered, tried to adjourn the meeting until the next morning, but Grandi leaped to his feet, shouting, "No, we have started this business, and we must finish it now." The voting took place at 2 A.M. Nineteen members of the Fascist Countil voted "Yes" in support of Grandi, seven voted "No," and two abstained. The meeting ended. At night, arrangements were made by the police and the carabinieris for Mussolini's arrest.

Mussolini spent the morning of Sunday, July 25, at his office in Rome. He asked to see the king and was granted an audience at 5 P.M. Upon entering the palace, he noticed large numbers of carabinieris in the yard. After they entered the drawing room, the king said, "My dear Duce, it's no longer any good. Italy has gone to bits; army morale is very low. The soldiers don't want to fight anymore . . . At this moment you are the most hated man in Italy. You have one friend left, and I am he. I will ensure your personal safety . . ." Mussolini tried to convince the king that he was making a mistake, but to no avail. The king accompanied the Duce to the door. A carabinieri captain stopped Mussolini and said, "His Majesty charged me with the protection of your person." He led Mussolini to an ambulance which took him to a house in Rome, and from there to the island of Ponza.

Following Mussolini's arrest, Marshal Badoglio, with the as-sistance of the Italian king, formed a new Italian government and immediately opened contacts with the British and Americans in order to arrive at a peace agreement with the Allies. Churchill and Roosevelt took immediate advantage of this fortuitous turn of events, and asked for surrender of all Italian forces including the still powerful Italian fleet, while promising easy peace terms and good treatment for the Italian people. It was very important for the Allies to capture the Italian fleet. This would make the Mediterranean, in effect, an Allied lake.

Hitler and his generals were stunned by this entire course of events. They didn't expect Mussolini would lose his power so quickly, and found themselves in a situation which was very dangerous and could easily turn into a disaster of major proportions. The German and Italian armed forces were intermingled on the Italian peninsula, and if the Allies could have obtained control of all Italy quickly, hundreds of thousands of German troops would have been trapped. The Allied forces would, in a short time, be right at the doorsteps of Austria.

To his credit, Hitler acted firmly and quickly. When the Italian fleet, in accordance with the Allied instructions, left Geneva and Spezia to surrender to the British at Malta, it was attacked on the way by German aircraft west of Sardinia. The battleship *Rome* was sunk and the battleship *Italia* sustained heavy damage. The rest of the fleet succeeded in reaching Malta. More importantly, the Germans quickly dispatched new divisions to Italy and occupied Rome, and areas north and south of it, thus creating an important buffer between central and western Europe, and the oncoming Allied forces which were in Italy fighting their way northward.

The landings at Salerno on September 9, 1943, were initially heavily opposed by the Germans, but the Allied forces were able to break out and unite with the armies advancing from the south.

Mussolini was taken from the island of Ponza to another island, La Maddalena, off the coast of Sardinia. From there, Marshal Badoglio had him moved to a mountain resort in the Abruzzi area of central Italy. Hitler, in need of a dramatic gesture to restore his prestige, gambled and won on a high risk rescue venture of Il Duce. On Sunday morning, September 12, 1943, ninety German parachutists landed near the hotel where Mussolini was kept prisoner. The Italian carabinieri got confused and offered no resistance. The stunned Duce was taken to a light German aircraft and flown to a meeting in Munich with his old pal, Hitler. This daring rescue, which was reminiscent of some high adventure movies, helped Hitler psychologically, but not materially. Mussolini set up a new puppet government, but the Italian people knew he was fighting a losing battle, and they were no longer prepared to risk their lives for him. Italy became a battleground where foreign armies were waging war on each other, while the Italian cities and villages were being destroyed and many of its people killed.

Abram and his unit continued to serve the VIIIth Army by supplying the front lines with munitions and other necessities and repairing military vehicles. The mood of the Jews in Unit 178 had improved considerably. They no longer had to worry about the threat that Rommel's Africa Corps posed to their homes and loved ones. They now knew that with Hitler's defeats in Russia, North Africa, and Sicily, the Allies were going to win the war. They were happy that they could play a part in the destruction of their enemy. They were eager to move on and see the German armies defeated. They were hoping that by volunteering and risking their lives in the Allied cause, they would gain the goodwill of the British people and be given a chance to establish their own Jewish State in Palestine.

The Italian terrain south of Rome was well suited for the defenders. The Germans took advantage of the mountainous area and offered stiff resistance to the oncoming Allies. It wasn't until the end of September that the American VIth Corps reached Naples. The cost of this advance was heavy. The Americans sustained 7,000 casualties and the British 5,000. The people of Naples greeted the American soldiers with flowers and joy. The Yanks were good-natured, many of them were of Italian descent. They were dispensing candy, chocolate, and other goodies to the starving Italians. Many of them were happy to be with the victorious Americans, especially the women. Thousands of children, fathered by American soldiers, were born later. A few of these romances resulted in marriage, but most girls were left behind without the fathers ever finding out that they had a son or a daughter in Italy.

The Germans had withdrawn to a line behind the Volturno River. Rainy weather set in and, combined with bad roads, it put a brake on the Allied advance. The Volturno line was held by three German divisions and was attacked by the Vth Army on October 12. Marshal Kesselring put up stiff resistance against the Americans and the British Xth Corps, which was attacking on the Allied right flank. Finally, the Germans were forced to withdraw to their next line of defense at the Gariglano River and the rugged hills further east.

The initial attacks on the new line were unsuccessful, and General Clark pulled back his forces and attacked again in the first week of December. Hitler was impressed by the stiff resistance his troops were offering to the Allies, and decided to reinforce them further with reserves stationed in northern Italy. He dissolved Rommel's Army Group and placed all German units in Italy under the command of Marshal Kesselring, who was proving that he was able to slow the Allied march down to a walk.

Hitler was hoping to delay the Allied capture of Rome for as long as possible because of the psychological effect the fall of this great city would have had. Both Montgomery and Clark found the going rough against the newly reinforced Germans.

The invasion of Italy was disappointing so far. It took the Allied Forces four months to advance seventy miles, and it cost them 60,000–70,000 casualties, far exceeding those sustained by the Germans who were helped by their strong man-made and natural defenses. It seemed now that the Allied planners of the Italian campaign did not do a very good job. Many military observers thought that the Allies should have landed north of Rome instead of at Salerno. Such landings would have been more surprising to the Germans, and the terrain north of Rome was better suited for offensive operations.

There was a basic disagreement between the Americans and the British on strategy leading to the liberation of Europe. The Americans felt that top priority should be given to the forthcoming landings across the English Channel without much concern about the Italian front. They considered it to be of peripheral importance, not being in the heart of the continent. The British, primarily Churchill, felt that reinforcing the Italian front would draw German reserves away from the German forces in France and Russia.

In all fairness, perhaps political consideration played a part in Churchill's judgment. He thought that with a quick conquest of Italy, it would have been easy to move the Allied forces from there to the Balkans, and thus prevent the Russians from playing a decisive role in that region's post-war developments.

The Allied command decided that a landing at Anzio, about fifty miles north of the Gustav Line which ran through the Gariglano River east through Monte Cassino, would draw the German forces from that line and render it easier to breach. The landing took place on January 22, 1944. Initially there was not much resistance, but the German reaction was quick and decisive. The Hermann Goering Division was switched northward and other units were sent in from Rome. In addition, more divisions to oppose the landings were available in northern Italy. Within a week, elements of eight German divisions were brought to Anzio. The German counterattack, supported by the Luftwaffe, began on February 16. Their soldiers breached the Allied defense perimeter and, for a while, the entire beachhead with tens of thousands of

American soldiers was in danger of being overrun. Fortunately, the lack of good roads slowed down the German attack and, helped by artillery, naval and air attacks, the Allies were able to hold their ground. Hitler ordered another attack on February 28, but this time, helped by good weather, and Allied air forces inflicted heavy damage on the attackers, and a stalemate developed.

On the Gustav Line itself, the German position on Monte Cassino proved most difficult to take. The New Zealand division, helped by massive artillery and air attacks, repeatedly attacked the elite German First Parachute Division, but it was stopped as well as were the new British infantry units. The Indian IVth Division attacked, but was stopped by a rain deluge which came in time to help the defenders. This was the third battle for Monte Cassino and all to no avail. The Cassino front was taken over by the British 78th Division and parts of the VIth Armored Division. The new offensive had to be delayed until May 11.

The VIIIth Army was given the main role, but the American Vth Army was to assist it by crossing the Gariglano River further east. The Americans on the Anzio beachhead were to break out, putting additional pressure on the Germans. This time the Polish corps consisting of two divisions was given the assignment to take Cassino. The Poles under General Anders took heavy casualties, pressed their attack, and finally captured the hill with its monastery on May 18. Thus came to an end one of the most ferocious battles of World War II, ranking with Stalingrad and Iwo Jima in intensity and bravery of both the attackers and the defenders. The Poles were proud of being able to accomplish what British Army units failed to do. They were hoping that their bravery and sacrifices would help them in establishing an independent Polish state at the end of the war. These hopes were not fulfilled as political considerations and the power of the Soviet army were instrumental in setting up a

puppet Polish government under Soviet control. It wasn't until
Gorbachev and his *perestroika,* which eventually led to the loos-
ening of the Soviet grip on their neighboring states, that the establishment of a truly independent Polish state became a
reality.

The fall of Monte Cassino coincided with the weakening of
the entire Gustav Line and the eventual fall of it. There was
hope that with the German retreat, the Allies would cut off the
German Xth Army which was holding the Gustav Line, but it
was able to extricate itself. The Germans put up temporary resistance south of Rome, but to no avail; and this great city fell
into Allied hands on June 4, 1944, two days before the invasion
of Normandy. To his credit, Kesselring declared Rome an
"open city" and thus, the destruction of this historical and
beautiful Italian capital was avoided.

The Germans now formed a new defensive line in Italy just
north of Florence, which was called the Gothic Line. It was attacked by the Allied armies on August 25. About the same time,
the American forces in Normandy achieved their breakthrough in France at St. Lo, and were on their way to liberate
Paris.

An important event took place in Abram's unit 178. Until
then it and the other Jewish units were an integral part of the
British Army. Now they were told that they would be integrated
into the Jewish Brigade. This Brigade was kept in Palestine during most of the war, and consisted of about 4,000 men, mostly
members of the Haganah. The brigade was sent to Tripoli to receive additional training, and after that to Fiuggi in the mountains of Italy. Abram's unit was ordered to move first to Fiuggi,
then to Vasto, Termoli, Ancona, Signa (Florence area), Rome,
Foggia, and back to Fiuggi. Finally, it was incorporated into the
Jewish Brigade at Acona on the Adriatic Sea. The American Vth
Army, fighting in northern Italy, ran short of transport vehicles,
and the services of Abram and his men were offered by the

British VIIIth Army in order to help their American allies. The fact that they, and no other transport unit, were sent was a great compliment to them because this meant that they were considered to be the best of all the transport units of the VIIIth Army.

Abram loved his new assignment. He and his soldiers were proud to have been chosen and eager to show the Americans how good they were. They were supplying the Vth Army that was attempting to overrun the last German defensive line south of Bologna and Argenta as a prelude to the final breakthrough into the northern Italian Po valley. This was the last offensive of the Italian campaign. It was launched on April 9, 1945, by the British and on April 14 by the Americans. It was a rout. The Americans broke through first and took Verona on April 26. The New Zealanders entered Venice on April 29.

Abram's unit was following the American front line closely as it was pushing the retreating Germans northward. When the German troops started to surrender, Abram and his transport unit rejoined the Jewish Brigade at Fiuggi. It spent the last few weeks of the war fighting the Germans in northeast Italy. They captured Ravenna, took many German prisoners, but lost thirty-eight men during the attack. These brave soldiers were buried with military honors in the Ravenna cemetery.

The war's end found Abram in a small village, Merciano, near Ravenna. Everybody was going crazy with joy. But there was much uncertainty and many tears. After years of fighting, seeing many of their comrades killed in action, it was hard to absorb in one big gulp that the war was over.

On April 25 a general uprising by the Italian people took place. Now the Italian soldiers were attacking the Germans as well. The Germans were surrendering everywhere. On April 28 Mussolini and his mistress, Claretta Petacci, were captured near Lake Como. Claretta stood by her long-time lover to the bitter end, even though she knew it would most likely cost her her life. Il Duce and Claretta were executed by their captors.

Their bodies were brought to Milan and strung up heads-down on meat hooks on the Piazza Loretta — the very spot where a group of Italian partisans was executed by the members of the small fascist forces still loyal to Mussolini only a couple of weeks before.

～ 13 ～

WORLD WAR II ENDS —
RECOVERY BEGINS

As exciting as the Italian campaign was for Abram, it played out against events of even greater importance to the outcome of World War II. The Russians, who by any measure played the most important role in Hitler's defeat, first halted the German invaders deep inside Russia and then turned the tables on their tormentors. They learned how to produce weapons as effective as any the Germans possessed. The weapons, generously supplied by the American people, were of great help as well. They learned new, modern military tactics and dealt the Nazi invaders defeat after defeat. The same soldiers that the Germans considered "untermentchen" (subhuman) made their oppressors tremble with fear whenever they had to serve at the Russian front. The Russians drove the Germans out of Russia, Poland, Romania, Bulgaria, Hungary, and Czecholsovakia. They broke into Germany, surrounded Berlin, and took the German capital in a massive and costly assault. They planted the Soviet flag on top of the German Reichstag, the very symbol of the hated Nazi regime. While doing all this, most of them showed great humanity. Even though the Germans terrorized the Russian civilians under their occupation and killed about

20 million of them, the Russians, when it was time for revenge, showed a great nobility of the Russian soul. It was very tempting for the Russian soldiers to kill millions of Germans during their victorious drive for Berlin, but they didn't do it. There were some isolated incidents of shooting, and many rapes, as happens with any invading army.

After the capture of Berlin, the Russians were eagerly looking for the arch-Devil himself, Adolf Hitler, but he cowardly eluded facing them, and the whole world as well, by taking his life in his bunker on April 29 — his mistress, Eva Braun, also committed suicide. (He married her in the last hours of their lives.) Their charred remains were found outside his Berlin bunker.

The Allies on the western front also did well in bringing about the German surrender which officially took place on May 8, 1945. They swept through West Germany with Patton's troops securing the first crossing of the Rhine by capturing the Remagen Bridge, with both Americans in the south and British in the north meeting little or no resistance. The first meeting of the Allied and Russian troops took place at Torgau when American and Russian soldiers shook hands and drank vodka. The world was rejoicing in the defeat of the Nazis, although a few more months went by before Japan surrendered in August, after the two atomic bombs were dropped on Hiroshima and Nagasaki causing hundreds of thousands of casualties.

President Roosevelt didn't live to see the end of the war. He died suddenly on April 12, 1945. He played a key part in the Nazi defeat, having to overcome the objections of American isolationists, who were against sending any help to save Great Britain. Many prominent Americans, including Charles Lindbergh and Joseph Kennedy, then Ambassador to Great Britain, were sympathetic to Hitler, but fortunately their views did not prevail.

All these momentous developments left Abram somewhat in shock. His mind was in turmoil. First of all, his thoughts were in Hrubieszow. He knew about the slaughter of Jews in all countries occupied by the Nazis. The first detailed account he received was from a French Jew who escaped from a concentration camp. One day as Abram was driving a truck at the Austrian frontier, a man jumped out of a ditch. He wore a striped uniform and was obviously sick. He approached Abram and said, "Can you help me? Please contact my friends in France. I was Leon Blum's (a French premier in prewar France) secretary." Abram told the man to get into the truck. He was on the way to Rotterdam, Holland, where he was to set up quarters for the Jewish Brigade, so he didn't have too much time. He took the man back to his unit and asked his soldiers to help the survivor.

The man told Abram what had happened to the Jews of Europe. Abram was aghast hearing of the murders of millions of innocent children, women, old people — everybody. The enormity of the disaster was hard to absorb. He knew now that his parents were probably dead, but was hoping that his younger brother, Chaim (Hy), somehow managed to survive.

As far as Palestine was concerned, everything was in flux. Nobody knew what the English were going to do. Abram and other soldiers of the Jewish Brigade were hoping that their contributions to the Allied victory would prove to be helpful in establishing a Jewish State in the Holy Land.

On the way to Holland they travelled through Austria, Germany, France, and Belgium. At one point they passed a German tank unit, still with heavy weapons, on the way to surrender. Abram's truck had a big Star of David painted on it, and for a moment, they were afraid that some crazy German might take a shot at them, but apparently the Germans were very demoralized, and all they could think of was how to get home. In Rotterdam they contacted the town's mayor and were assigned a barracks to house the Jewish Brigade.

Abram was told by one of the soldiers that nearby, in Germany, there was a large concentration camp, Bergen Belsen, and that there were thousands of survivors still there. He took a jeep and his driver and went to see the camp. He stopped at Celle, which was three miles from Bergen Belsen. In Celle he asked one of the Germans to tell him where Bergen Belsen was. The man said he didn't know. With the help of a map, Abram found the place. A Hungarian Nazi S.S. auxiliary unit was guarding the camp. The German S.S. was gone.

Abram drove through the gates. Apparently he was the first Jewish-English soldier with a Star of David showing to visit the camp. A number of women and a few men came out and surrounded the jeep. All of them looked like skeletons, they had no hair, their eyes were feverish, and most could barely walk. A few warned Abram, "Don't touch us, we have typhoid fever." Abram asked the people around him, "Do you know if there is anyone here from Hrubieszow?" An emaciated woman approached the jeep and said, "I'm Hela Furst." She recognized Abram, but he wasn't able to recognize her. She was emaciated and was crying. Abram couldn't believe his eyes, he had known her as a girl in Hrubieszow. She was a pretty girl with beautiful, dark eyes; a few years younger than Abram and attended the same gymnazjum. Hela told Abram what happened to the Hrubieszow Jews. His parents were killed by the Nazis and that his father, Fishel, was in fact shot together with her father and they were buried together. His younger brother, Hy, was taken to a concentration camp in Germany, but she didn't know which one or if he was alive.

Even though, by now, Abram was suspecting the worst, the confirmation of his parents' brutal murder was hard to accept. But at least there was hope that Hy was alive. He knew immediately that searching for his brother was a high priority in his life. But for now, Abram had to hurry back to Amsterdam because he had to take care of final details concerning the movement of the Jewish Brigade to its new quarters. He left all the food he had with him for the ex-prisoners and told Hela he would be back soon. On his way back he could hardly contain his rage at the thought of what the Nazis did to his family and other innocent Jews. He stopped in Celle, and in the middle of a crowded street he asked one of the Germans to tell him where Bergen Belsen is. The man answered in German, "Ich weis nicht." (I don't know.) Abram hit him on the head with the butt of his gun, and the German fell bleeding to the ground. Two English military policemen came over and asked, "What happened, Captain?" "Nothing," replied Abram. "He just didn't know where Bergen Belsen is."

Two days later Abram went back to the camp again. He talked to Hela again. This time he brought a lot of food with him, but she told him it wasn't really needed, as they were getting plenty of food from English soldiers. The biggest problem was that many of the former inmates ate too much in the days immediately after the liberation and were sick with dysentery. Some of them died because of it. Others were dying because they were too weak to recover from the beatings and hunger of the concentration camps. Hela herself had typhoid fever and was hardly able to stand. There was another man among the people, Pinchas, who used to drive a droshka (a horse-driven taxi cab) in Hrubieszow and whom Abram remembered quite well. Both Hela and Pinchas told Abram that they would never go back to Poland to live and described how most of the Poles had enjoyed watching the killings of their Jewish neighbors.

Abram went back to Italy so that he could accompany the Brigade to its new quarters in Rotterdam. It was the end of July. The weather was beautiful, and as they were passing through Austria and Germany again, they enjoyed the furtive looks the German men and women were giving the column of trucks with big Stars of David on them. Everything was still topsy-turvy in the aftermath of the war. In Germany there were millions of Allied soldiers, survivors of concentration camps, and slave workers brought in from all over Europe to work in German factories during the war. Hundreds of thousands of people were jamming the roads on the way back to their native countries. Others were trying to find temporary shelter in Germany itself.

Once in Rotterdam the men of the Jewish Brigade settled into their new quarters. Abram and his transport unit were given the task of supplying all the British troops in Holland. The Dutch were extremely friendly to the British Army soldiers. The Dutch, as a people, have distinguished themselves by showing their great humanity during the German occupation. More than any other people of Europe (the Danes were very helpful too), they saved their fellow citizen Jews by helping them to hide, often risking their own lives by doing so. Thousands of Dutch Jews survived because this generosity of spirit of their countrymen. There was, however, a small segment of the population that was cooperating with the Nazis, and thousands of young Dutchmen volunteered to serve in special Dutch units that were fighting alongside the Germans. But they were despised by the majority of Dutchmen and were considered to be traitors.

The Dutch girls, perhaps because there was a shortage of men during the war, were pursuing English soldiers and they, of course, had a field day as far as finding female company was concerned. In England it was customary for men to pursue the women but here, to their delight, it was the other way around. And it wasn't that the girls were looking for food and gifts; they actually loved the company of British soldiers. Abram, a tall, handsome man, looked very attractive in his English Army Captain's uniform and had his choice of many beautiful Dutch young ladies.

Abram's unit received orders to move from Rotterdam to Leuse, near Mons, on the French-Belgian frontier. They were transporting English soldiers who were going home on leave via Calais, and also delivering provisions to various British Army units. Then they were moved in rapid succession to The Hague, to Schevnningen, where they visited the launching pads for V2s which killed many people in England, and then to Breda, all in Holland. Unexpectedly, in Breda, Abram received good news. He was promoted to Major. This was a great honor especially for a Palestinian Jew who enlisted as a private and, because of his exceptional courage and ability, earned this new rank. Abram and his friends celebrated his new title late into the night.

~ 14 ~

SEARCHING FOR HY

From the time Abram heard from Hela Furst that Hy was sent to concentration camps, he couldn't stop thinking about him.

It was July 1945. He had no clue as to where Hy could be. As the days went by, the feeling that Hy was alive and that he would find him became almost an obsession. He couldn't sleep at night, and he actually felt Hy's presence around him. His fellow officers thought that he had gone crazy, but Abram wouldn't listen to anyone.

He went to see his superior officer and asked for a leave, but found that it wasn't easy to get. The commanding officer told him, "We need you here now. We are busy." He asked, "Do you have any specific information that he is alive?" Abram said, "No, but in my heart I know he is, and I have to find him." The officer sensed that Abram would go even without leave, and granted him one.

Abram made arrangements for a station wagon, an English Fordson, and got a German-Jewish young man in his unit to be his driver. He procured what he knew Hy would need: a British Army uniform, boots, fake British soldier's papers. He went to a British Intelligence Office and obtained a map marked with the locations of about sixty DP camps in Germany.

Abram and his driver went to former concentration and labor camps, and DP camps, perhaps about twenty in all. In the DP camps the officials had lists of their people so it didn't take long to find a few survivors who were from other towns but knew his father, Fishel, because of his prewar activities in the national headquarters of the Keren Hajesod. However, he was unable to find anyone from Hrubieszow itself.

After nine days of driving from camp to camp, they reached Munich. They were told that there may be some Jews in a camp on the outskirts of Egenfelden. Abram's driver told him that he was dead tired and that he must have some rest. Abram, who was himself completely exhausted, did not want to wait, so he took over the driving to Egenfelden.

As soon as they reached the town, they stopped at the first house. Abram knocked at the door. A middle-aged German man opened the door. He looked scared when he saw a British officer. "What do you want," he asked. Abram said, "Where is the DP camp?" The man said it was about 1 kilometer away. Abram pulled out his pistol and told the German to take him there. The man's wife, suspecting the worst, followed them crying. Abram and the Germans walked; the driver in the jeep followed them.

An American patrol stopped them. "Where are you going, Limey," one of them asked. When told they were going to the DP camp, the Americans drove away. They reached the camp and went through the gate. The German asked, "Can I go home now?" Abram told him, "Go." A light was on in one of the barracks. Abram knocked at the door. Someone opened it, and Abram saw a few men sitting around a table playing cards. They were Poles who were brought to Germany as forced laborers. "Are there any Jews in the camp," asked Abram in Polish. The Poles were visibly surprised hearing a British Army Major speaking their native tongue. "Not anymore," one of the Poles said. "They moved to Egenfelden." "Do you know if there were any Jews from Hrubieszow there," Abram asked. They didn't know. Abram, in desperation said, "D you know any of those men's names?" They said they knew one nice young man called Chaimek by his friends. (Chaimek is a diminutive for Chaim — Hy's Jewish name.) "What does he look like?" Abram asked. The Pole said, "A little taller than you."

One of the Poles, impressed by the British officer, offered to accompany them to town. Once there he pointed to a house and said, "Chaimek lives here on the second floor." Abram was now all nerves. The tension was unbearable. He sat down on the pavement, and told the Pole, "Do me a favor, go up and tell the Jews, that the Palestinians have come to visit them." The Pole soon came down accompanied by a Jewish man. He told Abram his name was Lejbele Bernstein, and that he was from Hrubieszow. Abram didn't remember ever seeing him. Another man appeared in the second floor window, and seeing a British officer hollered, "Er sicht a kurve?" (In Yiddish — Is he looking for a whore?") Lejbele asked Abram, "Who are you looking for?" Chaim Silberstein, my brother," said Abram. Bernstein's eyes lit up. "He's here," he said, "He just came back from Prague. He told me he had a brother in Palestine." Abram ran upstairs — Hy was there. All Abram remembers is that they embraced. The emotion and exhaustion finally got the better of him. He passed out and sank to the floor.

He woke up in the morning and there was Hy, who had been sitting next to him all night crying from joy. Hy told him he had left Egenfelden a week before to go back to Poland, but changed his mind when he was walking on a street in Prague and ran into a friend of his, Henry Orenstein, a young Jew from Hrubieszow. Henry told him about the new pogroms in many Polish towns where Poles killed many Jews, and urged him not

to go back to Poland as there was no future for Jews there. Hy
had returned to Egenfelden just hours before.

The brothers were too emotional to be able to talk about
their parents and how they were killed. Abram showed Hy the
uniform he brought for him and the identity papers, and said,
"Get going, you are coming with me." Hy hesitated and was
clearly unsure of himself. "I don't know if I can leave now," he
said. "I'm working with American Intelligence." There was an
American Intelligence officer who was taken prisoner by the
Germans during the war who was now in charge of the local intelligence unit. He took a real liking to Hy and used him to
help find former Nazis. Abram could tell that Hy still had not
fully recovered from the horrors of the concentration camps
and that he needed help, so he decided to take matters into his
own hands.

The next day he went with Hy to pay the American a visit.
The officer told Abram that he and his family lived in Chicago
and that he wanted to take Hy back home with him and make
him part of his family. Abram told the officer how much he appreciated everything he was doing for Hy, but that the two of
them were the only ones from the immediate family left alive,
that their future was in Palestine where eventually they were
hoping to have a Jewish homeland. The officer understood and
reluctantly he agreed with Abram.

Abram noticed that Hy's teeth were loose and his gums in-
fected, apparently caused by years of malnutrition. He took Hy
to a local German doctor who said that it would be best for Hy
to have all his teeth pulled out to stop the infection. When
questioned further, the doctor said, "Well, you English have
this new miracle drug, penicillin, perhaps that would help. We
don't have any here in Germany, but you are a British officer,
maybe you will be able to get it." Abram could tell that Hy, in
addition to his gum infection, was not in very good shape physically or emotionally. Abram decided that the best thing would

be for them both to go back to Holland where he knew many people and would be in a better position to get help.

The American officer, Hy, and his friends were all crying when they said good-bye to each other. Abram offered to take a few of Hy's close friends to Holland, but they all said they wanted to go to America.

They travelled to Holland and Abram put Hy in a military hospital. Penicillin was very scarce, so Abram arranged a meeting with the British Colonel in charge, and after a lengthy discussion, the Colonel agreed to supply the drug. Hy stayed in the hospital for two weeks. The penicillin worked wonders. Hy left the hospital with his teeth in pretty good shape.

Abram knew how important it was to help Hy recover from his psychological wounds. They went to the best restaurants. They were surrounded by beautiful Dutch girls. Hy was also a very handsome, tall young man and girls were flocking to them both in droves. They were especially attracted by Abram's British Army Major's uniform. Whenever Abram's mission with the refugees took him to France or Italy, the girls were eager to meet him, giving him long looks and sending little notes.

One day he and Hy were walking down a Rotterdam street when a beautiful, tall blond young woman passed them. Hy gave her an admiring look. Abram noticed that and said, "Watch." He followed the young lady, introduced himself. She was the daughter of a general in the Swedish Red Cross. The Swedish Red Cross under Count Bernadette distinguished itself in the last days of World War II by succeeding in getting permission from Himmler to send dozens of trucks loaded with food to meet concentration camp prisoners and feed them during the "death marches" after the camps were evacuated.

Abram and the lady — Abram prefers not to mention her name — became friends, and spent a lot of time together in the following months.

After six weeks in Holland, Abram felt that Hy had recovered quite well and arranged for him to go to Palestine. He wanted Hy to be with their remaining family and get a feeling of belonging. He procured an English sergeant's papers for Hy, and got him into a group that was going to Palestine on leave. They travelled to Marseilles, to Egypt, and finally to Tel Aviv. Hy stayed with Aunt Clara and sent his fake sergeant's papers back to Abram. He began to learn Hebrew and to adjust to a more normal life.

∾ 15 ∾

A NEW MISSION — SENDING
SURVIVORS TO PALESTINE

A new, important development in Abram's life now took place. Soon after the end of the war, the Haganah took over the leadership of relocating tens of thousands of surviving Jews in central and western Europe who wished to go to Palestine. A few hundred thousand Jews from Germany, Poland, Romania, Hungary, Czechoslovakia, or the U.S.S.R. survived the Holocaust in concentration camps or in hiding and were now living in Displaced Persons Camps or in temporary shelters. Most of them, having experienced the anti-Semitism of the people in their native lands, didn't want to stay in Europe. Many wanted to emigrate to the United States and make a new life for themselves in that exciting country they heard so much about. But many others were yearning to finally find a real home of their own, to go to Palestine hoping that eventually Jews will be able to establish their own state there.

The Palestinian Jews were anxious to get most of the survivors to Palestine. They wanted to take care of their brothers and sisters who suffered so much, but were motivated also by the knowledge that in order to be able to claim and establish their own country, they would have to fight for it. They needed more people to counterbalance the threat of millions of Arabs. The Arabs wanted nothing less than to get rid of all the Jews in Palestine and create their own state there.

The Haganah set up the headquarters for this operation in Paris and soon contacted Abram, who they knew was instrumental in shipping thousands of weapons from Egypt to Palestine, and had distinguished himself fighting the Germans during the war. They were buying or leasing old ships, planning to use them to transport tens of thousands of surviving Jews to Palestine from ports in Italy and southern France.

Abram went to Paris and met with Ehod Avriel, one of the Haganah leaders, in a small hotel near Place d'Etoile. Avriel told him that it was their responsibility to save the refugees. "This is a critical hour," he said. He wanted Abram to be in charge of transporting the refugees from northern Europe. The Haganah people knew that he was in command of a truck unit and that his trucks were being used to make deliveries to many British units in northern Europe. Avriel asked Abram to arrange a meeting with all the majors of the Jewish Brigade in order to enlist their help in this operation.

When Abram returned to Breda he asked ten Jewish officers, all of them majors, to come to the meeting. Abram expected some resistance to the idea of working with the Haganah, but was shocked when all ten refused to participate in the operation. One by one they got up and told him that they could not get mixed up in this operation. It was too dangerous. The British were liable to find out about it, and there would be hell to pay. They wanted nothing to distract the return of the Jewish Brigade to Palestine with a good record, etc., etc. Abram tried to explain how critical this operation was, but to no avail. They were just afraid to lose their ranks.

He went back to Paris and told the Haganah people, "Forget these people; I will do the job myself." Later, Karu wrote in his memoirs how astonished he was that Abram would risk prison and disgrace in the British Army to do this job. Abram picked out a few of his subordinates whom he felt he could trust with Moshe Karu, the R.S.M. of the 178th Unit as the leader.

While in The Hague, he saw many Dutch trucks that were parked and unattended. He and his men started stealing them, one by one, then they would immediately repair them and change a few parts so that they wouldn't be easily recognizable. They changed the truck numbers so each of them had the same number as one of the trucks in Abram's unit. They visited a few refugee camps and picked out a number of young men who were eager to participate and quick to learn.

They obtained false British Army driver's licenses that were duplicates of those held by some of the men in Abram's unit. They gave the young men British Army uniforms and taught them how to drive.

The Haganah in Paris was responsible for the overall coordination of Abram's operation. Soldiers from Abram's unit drove the stolen trucks to various Displaced Persons (DP) camps in Germany, including one in Landsberg and one near Munich. The Haganah men, together with some of the people they recruited in the camps, had lists of the refugees who were ready to go and waiting to be picked up, usually at night. The young refugees were helpful in driving the trucks for local deliveries.

There was a parallel operation in Italy similar to the one Abram created in northern Europe. The Italian organization was headed by Officers Nahmias, Shmorag, and Buganov, who were part of the Jewish Transport Unit serving in Italy. This unit was also part of the British Army, but was not connected to the Jewish Brigade.

Of course everything had to be done in complete secrecy and it was difficult to maintain because so many people in so many places were involved. Jewish officers who organized and

implemented this scam were brave men who were fully aware
that since they were British Army officers, if caught, they would
have been quickly courtmartialed and most likely jailed for
stealing British property, falsifying documents, etc. They did it
because they knew that was the only way tens of thousands of
Jewish survivors would reach Palestine.

Each of these convoys consisted of ten to fifteen trucks,
each holding about twenty-five refugees dressed in British
Army uniforms. When Abram and his convoy would arrive at a
French frontier checkpoint, they would tell the French frontier
guards that they were taking English soldiers on leave to Calais
to be shipped home. After crossing the frontier, the refugees
changed their British Army uniforms for work clothing and
were holding picks and shovels pretending they were civilian
workers being taken to a military construction job. They would
be driven to Marseilles, loaded onto a waiting ship, and be on
their way to Palestine.

Soon the British authorities became aware that some unusual activities were taking place, but were not sure what was
going on. They instituted strict controls in their sector of the
French-German border and did not permit any truck movement at night. On one of the trips, the operation almost got
into real trouble.

Abram was awakened by a telephone call at 3 A.M. The
man in charge of the convoy told him that French guards
stopped them at the frontier and told him that they would
have to wait till 6 A.M. for inspection. Abram rushed to the
place and confronted the guards. He was very aggressive. He
hollered, "How dare you make British soldiers on leave going
home after the war wait for hours until your inspector is ready."
The head guard was apologetic, "Sorry, Sir, but your own
British military policemen told us not to let anyone through at
night."

Abram demanded to see the French officer in charge immediately. The guard said, "But he is now in bed with his mis-

tress." Abram insisted on seeing the officer at once anyway. The intimidated guard led Abram to a house. Abram knocked at the door. The officer opened it up holding up his pants with one hand. "What's going on," he demanded to know. Abram shouted, "How dare you hold up 500 British soldiers. Because of you they will miss the ship at Calais." The officer started to explain, "But your own police . . ." "Fuck the police," Abram interrupted. "I want my boys to go home now." The Frenchman was now visibly shaken. He was also embarrassed to be caught in this situation in front of the neighbors, who started looking out of the windows to see what was going on. He lamely told his subordinate to let the convoy pass, and their journey resumed.

They had to use all kinds of tricks. When they knew that a certain border inspection spot was especially dangerous, they would wait on the side of the road for a legitimate British convoy and mix in with them. As more and more Jews in the DP camps and other places were finding out that there was a way to get to Palestine through Marseilles, they started arriving there on their own by buses, trains, and some even on foot. They were mostly from camps in Germany, but many were coming from as far as Poland, Ukraine, and the Baltic countries. They were finding out that even after the horrors of the Holocaust, the great majority of their gentile neighbors didn't want them there. Some of the local people were motivated by greed, having occupied former Jewish homes and were not willing to give them up — others by pure hatred, bred into them by their priests and anti-Semitic agitators. Many of these Jewish survivors of concentration camps or hiding places had an overwhelming desire to finally have their own country — and a real home. The Haganah was straining to handle this great mass of people. Abram and his group alone were responsible for bringing tens of thousands of people to Marseilles. Karu wrote in his memoirs about a Dr. Mase who, on his own, transported a small number of Jews to Marseilles.

The following are excerpts from a book written by Moshe Karu, Secretary of Kibbutz Yakum, that throw additional light on Haganah activities in Europe, including these of Abram, to bring weapons and survivors to Palestine.

Translation of Hebrew excerpts from the book *Jewish Transport Units, British Army in the Desert and Europe, 1939–1945*:

The Quiet Blond Newcomer
page 201

The R.S.M. of the Second Battalion, J.B.G. Israel Carmi, introduced me to a blond R.S.M. by the name of Monia Meridor, a quiet man who didn't talk much. He was a civilian in disguise sent by the Haganah with the mission of buying weapons.

I took him under my wing and had to accompany him and guide him. There were many questions that were asked about him in the dining hall. I stopped it all by saying, "He is one of ours, don't worry." As his caretaker, I went with him to Paris to meet Nahum Shadmi, the Haganah's representative. A grand plan of getting weapons was laid out. Israel Carmi and Monia Meridor began touring the Brigade Units which kept guard over the army stores around Antwerp.

I was given the task of hoarding empty barrels, which were prepared by our workshops for the packing of arms. They had to be welded and then re-painted with the signs of the Red Cross. Those barrels had to be sent by trucks to Marseilles where the ship *Tel-Hay* was hiding in the docks. We toured the magazines and made final arrangements with the commanders to ensure that only trustworthy people will be on duty on the decisive night.

I went again with Monia Meridor to Paris where he disclosed to me at the Haganah H.Q. that Shadmi had in mind to propose to Major A. Silberstein to take over the management of all our activities and logistics concerning Jewish refugees in northern Europe. I had great doubt that Silberstein would concede to take on that heavy and dangerous burden. I was wrong in my judgment of Silberstein. He was invited to Paris for a meeting with the top heads, Nahum Shadmi, Ishak Levy, and the boss, Ehod Avriel (later Ambassador to the continent of Africa). They proposed to Silberstein to take over the management of all activities in the various units concerning the saving of refugees. He accepted the responsibility."

A Mild Response From the Majors
page 202

Silberstein, upon his return to Belgium, invited all the majors of the Brigade, asking them for support in the strenuous logistics of moving refugees from all over Europe to the south and northern ports. The meeting was a complete fiasco. They all gave negative replies, pointing out the danger to the Brigade and their personal risks as high officers at a time when the British Military Police kept a continuous watch over the area.

Understanding that there is nobody to rely on while the situation was extremely urgent, a grand scheme of daring thievery was put into immediate action. That produced thirty-four trucks of the same make that we were equipped with. These trucks were taken away from the freshly formed Dutch

Army, immediately repainted, marked and numbered in our workshops. Now we have two double platoons with the same numbers, but kept apart in different locations.

The trucks were driven by young refugees, whom we dressed as soldiers (with double names), and trained as drivers in our daily chores. When checked by the Military Police, their papers and work tickets were always correct. The real soldiers were given the difficult and illegal tasks, marked by us as T.T.G.

The evening before the arms had to be taken out from the magazines, Monia and Israel arrived with a new order. Instead of weapons, we had to carry refugees to the ship, *Tel-Hay*, the same ship that was destined before for the load of arms.

On June 3, 1946, a meeting was held in my room. Present were: Major Silberstein; C.S.M. Muller; M. Meridor; R.S.M. Israel Carmi, and myself. Sixteen trucks were needed for the operation. Twelve will be supplied by the 178th R.A.S.C., J.B.C., the remaining four will come (in spite of all) from the Brigade. Silberstein wasn't too happy with the size of the illegal convoy. He thought it was too big and too risky under the circumstances. After hesitation, he agreed on condition that I will accompany the convoy during the whole operation. It was decided that Israel Carmi would lead the convoy, while I would take on the technical responsibility.

Silberstein approached me saying, "In case of serious damage to a truck, burn it completely so that no visible sign would remain." To that I replied, "You really think that I shall destroy a truck, don't worry, they shall all return safely."

Racing South
page 203

Close to midnight on the 9.3.1946 the trucks, one by one, arrived to a house on the outskirts of Antwerp. In minutes they were filled up with young men and women, carrying single little bags. The tarpaulins were closed and strung up so that nothing could be seen from the outside. Every truck moved immediately towards Brussels. Israel Carmi led while I took up the rear. The race southward to France began on a rainy, foggy night with each truck containing thirty persons. The drivers had to interchange as the conditions were most straining because of high speed, bad roads and dense fog. Every two hours we stopped at the side of the road for people to relieve themselves, girls on the left and boys on the right.

We passed the French border, this time without difficulty, as Captain Deshalit informed officially the guard frontier station that an urgent convoy will pass that night. I was overtaking the trucks in my jeep, checking up on them and waited for them on the crossroads. We had some minor incidents and damage, but we overcame it. Another difficult night had passed and at dawn we reached Marseilles. Our trucks entered a DP camp. We pretended to be English to the French officials, and unloaded our people.

After handing over our transport to a secret Haganah agent on the spot, and after a good, quick French meal and refuelling, we turned back north. Tired but happy, the worries about our transport were behind us. Having driven more than thirty-six hours, we returned to our camp.

A short rest and nap, and we were ready for another sortie. I had to get a few new drivers because the ones from the Brigade weren't up to our standards.

Surprise
page 205

We took to the road again. Close to midnight we reached a farm on the Holland-Belgium frontier. We surprised a big group of youngsters, refugees in our care, who were sitting at tables singing. They didn't expect us at this late hour.

Suddenly one of the instructors got up, asked for silence, and in a quiet voice said, "All of you will go immediately to your rooms and come back here with your personal handbags. Outside trucks are waiting for you. You are starting a journey, at the end of which, I hope, we shall meet in Eretz (Palestine)."

They were hoping for this news for a long time. Still when it came, they were dumbfounded. There was complete silence. You could see some of them wiping their tears. I was watching from the side, and had to turn away not to be seen with tears in my eyes. I was profoundly moved. Fifteen minutes later the trucks were filled up with the happy youngsters ready to go. We left the Belgium-Dutch frontier at midnight and started another race of thirty-six hours southward . . ."

Some of the older ships the Haganah used didn't have bunks for people to sleep on during the passage, and Abram was asked for help. He was able to find a supply of wood planks which Haganah people used to make makeshift bunks. They were also very short of oil. Abram knew there was a large petrol base at Liege, so he went there, got acquainted with the guards who were patrolling the base, and soon invited them to a party. He brought lots of whisky, invited a number of Belgian girls, and kept the guards busy. While the party was in full swing, his people filled hundreds of barrels with oil and shipped them to Marseilles. He got so accustomed to stealing trucks and other supplies, that he sometimes tended to forget the great dangers he and his helpers were exposing themselves to.

∼ 16 ∼

NEW TROUBLES
WITH THE BRITISH

Things were heating up between the British government and the Palestinian Jews. One would have thought that considering the slaughter of 6,000,000 Jews of Europe, the British government would be more sympathetic to Jews and to Jewish immigration to Palestine. Another reason for that was the influence of the Jewish community in the U.S., might have in protecting Britain's relationship with the U.S. which was critically important to the war-exhausted country. But no such thing had happened. The Attlee government (which came to power after Labor's surprising victory over Churchill's Tories), decided not to make any major concessions on Jewish immigration to Palestine. The British Secretary of State, Ernest Bevin, who did not even try to conceal his anti-Jewish sentiment, publicly stated, "Jews must not try to get out to the head of the queue." This statement caused great concern to Jews everywhere. Considering the support given by most Arabs to Hitler and the sacrifices of Jewish soldiers in the British Army, this was viewed as cold political calculation, based less on justice and fairness, than the desire not to antagonize the Arabs because of oil and other economic considerations.

In Tel Aviv riots took place. Jewish crowds were fired upon by British soldiers. Six Jews were killed by British bullets. An Anglo-American committee of inquiry (into the Palestinian matter) made public its report in May 1946, recommending an immediate admission of 100,000 Jewish Holocaust survivors to Palestine. President Truman made a public statement calling on Britain to accept the committee's recommendations. All to no avail. The Attlee government refused to take any action until "the Jewish disarmament takes place." The mere thought that the Jews, surrounded by a bloodthirsty Arab population and an unfriendly British Army, would give up their weapons and leave themselves open to massacres was ridiculous.

In May 1946, Ernest Bevin told a British Labour Party conference that the reason why the Americans were pressing for so many Jews to be admitted to Palestine was that "they did not want them in New York."

But let's not get too far ahead in telling Abram's story. Abram's unit was moved from Holland to Calais. These were frustrating times. Abram was anxious to get back to Palestine because of the reports about unrest among the British, the Arabs, and the Jews. He was also worried about the British Intelligence discovering his role in moving tens of thousands of Jewish survivors to Palestine. After about a month in Calais, he was told that his unit was going to be shipped to Palestine.

Abram felt a great sense of relief. It appeared that he would be able to return to Palestine without any repercussions from his role in stealing thirty-four trucks from the Dutch, oil from the British Army, forging British documents, etc., and arranging the shipment of survivors to Marseilles. But this was not to be — not for him. One the morning of their departure, two British D.R.s appeared with a letter commanding Abram to go to Hildesheim, Germany. He went by train through Belgium, Holland, and into Germany. At a military installation near

Hildesheim, a British Intelligence officer informed him that he was kept for questioning.

Abram stayed at the Hildesheim installation for six weeks without being told why. These were difficult days for him. He couldn't take his mind off Palestine. He was anxious about reports of thousands of Jewish survivors being kept virtual prisoners on the island of Cyprus. He knew that in the days and months to come, momentous events would take place in Palestine, events that would decide the future of the Jewish community there, as well as of tens of thousands of other Jews being interned on Cyprus or still in Europe anxious to get to their new homeland. He was also concerned about Hy who he knew was having a hard time adjusting from the nightmare of concentration camps to his new life in Tel Aviv. The days dragged on endlessly. After six weeks he was told the reason for his arrest. He was accused of shipping Jewish survivors to French and Italian ports illegally using English military trucks. Interrogated every day, Abram, suspecting that his accusers had no definitive proof of his activity, firmly denied all their charges.

He and the other 400 British officers who were accused of a variety of crimes were treated well. The prisoners were able to ride horses, be visited by their girlfriends, and had plenty of whisky. One day Abram drank too much, got very sick, and had to stay in bed with his head wrapped in towels.

Finally, after ten more weeks, he was told that he was being sent to London. Upon his arrival at the War Office, an English Major greeted him, "Major Silberstein, sit down." He said, "Major, we know you were transporting the refugees, but we have no proof; go home." It was ironic that while all this interrogation was going on, Abram received a letter from Marshal Montgomery, the Commander-in-Chief of all British forces, commending him for unusual bravery during the African campaign. The Army gave him two weeks of paid leave in London, where he stayed in a hotel for British Army officers.

He spent his time in London visiting museums, art galleries, castles, the Tower of London, and other places of interest. One day he was standing in front of Buckingham Palace. The guards, seeing a British Army Major, jumped to salute him. He had a few American friends with him whom he had met in London. They all laughed, "Look at the fuss the guards make about you, Abram."

One incident Abram remembers well took place during breakfast at his hotel. An elderly British Colonel was sitting at a nearby table, cursing as he was reading a newspaper. Abram soon became aware that the Colonel was cursing Jews. Abram felt chills running through his body. He got up, went to the Colonel's table, and said aloud, "You bastard. I fought during the entire war for you so you can sit here in comfort on your ass in England. I am a Jew." Officers sitting at the other tables looked in amazement. The Colonel looked at Abram, dropped his paper on the table and ran out of the room. The other officers came over to Abram, shook his hands, and apologized for the old man.

Abram booked passage on a ship from London to Palestine. The rest of the Jewish Brigade had been home for quite a while. So, Abram Silberstein was the first Palestinian Jew to enlist in the British Army and the last to be discharged. He spent more time in the army than any other Palestinian. He rose from a private to the rank of a major. His contributions to the Allied war effort are told on these pages. His greatest contribution to the future state of Israel was to be vitally instrumental in stealing and shipping thousands of Italian weapons to Palestine. In 1946–1948 the Jews of Israel had very few weapons with which to fight the Arab armies and British soldiers. These Italian weapons were of enormous importance to Jewish survival in Palestine, and in the establishment of a Jewish State.

∾ 17 ∾

TURMOIL IN PALESTINE

Abram arrived in Palestine toward the end of 1946. He stayed with Hy and their Aunt Clara. His family was greatly relieved to see him. They couldn't understand why Abram was the only member of the Jewish Brigade to be detained in Europe for so long, and he couldn't tell them the reason in his letters because he was under investigation. He went to the British military base in Sarafand and received his honorable discharge.

He found Palestine in great turmoil. The Attlee government was still pursuing their anti-Jewish policies. The British military establishment was pushing their government to adopt harsh policies against the Jews. Their real goal was to maintain control of Palestine. They considered it a strategic key to the Middle East and didn't want to antagonize the neighboring Arab states. Of course, there was also the usual motivation of any military — the more territory they controlled, the more important their own role was to their nation.

The Jews knew very well that they lived in a decisive moment of their history. They were not interested in money; they were idealistic. They wanted their own national home, and they were prepared to do whatever it took to make their dreams come true. However, even with all their fighting spirit and readiness for sacrifice, the odds against them seemed insurmountable. Many thousands of them fought in World War II, but as they were being discharged, they had to surrender their weapons.

The Haganah was primarily a defensive organization equipped with obsolete weapons. Its primary goal was to defend Jews from Arab attacks. As Ben-Gurion told the Anglo-American committee of inquiry, "Haganah is a Hebrew word for 'defense.'" The Haganah developed the Palmach, an underground military unit with about 10,000 members. Menachem Begin, who was a disciple of Vladimir Zabotinsky and believed that Jews would succeed in establishing a Jewish State only through an armed struggle, organized the Etzel (Irgun) which was about 2,000–3,000 strong. Etzel's policy was to fight the British as well as the Arabs. Stern was the head of another unit called the Lehi (the British referred to them as the "Stern Gang"). They considered the English to be their primary enemy and confined their attacks to British targets. British soldiers succeeded in killing Stern and Itzchak Shamir took over the leadership of the unit.

The Arabs were relatively quiet in this period, perhaps they believed that after the English and the Jews got worn out by fighting each other, they would step in and take over. The Attlee government, undoubtedly again under pressure from their military, authorized the Palestine High Commissioner, Sir Alan Cunningham, to crack down on the Jewish political and military leadership. Thousands of Jews were arrested (Ben-Gurion escaped arrest because he happened to be outside the country at the time.) Extensive searches were conducted by the British military. For weeks Palestine was virtually under military siege.

The British government lost all its confidence in the Jewish Agency. The Agency leaders, especially Ben-Gurion, were officially cooperating with the British, but actually were in control of at least some of the Jewish military forces, especially the Haganah and the Palmach. They even refused to cooperate with the British against the Irgun and the Lehi, whose policies they disagreed with. They were all Jews, and even though they employed different methods, their goals were basically the same. Ben-Gurion, especially, was forced by circumstances to wear two masks. He was negotiating and pleading the Jewish cause with the British, while at the same time, meeting with clandestine Jewish military leaders and organizing a flow of supplies to them.

Now the American Jews and their friends in the U.S. government and Congress became outraged by the brutal British military tactics, and began to apply pressure on Britain, which needed large loans from America to rebuild their war-weakened Empire. Dr. Abba Hillel Silver, an American Zionist leader, asked his followers to lean on their elected representatives to deny American loans to Britain. The British government began to realize that major damage could be done to Britain by continuing their aggressive anti-Jewish policies in Israel, and by the end of 1946 ordered its military to discontinue their extreme measures against the Jewish Agency and the Haganah.

Until then, the British military considered the Haganah their main enemy. They changed their minds when in July 1947, the Irgun blew up the King David Hotel in Jerusalem. Eighty British, Jewish, and Arab civil servants were killed and seventy wounded (mostly British), and government offices destroyed. The British imposed a four-day curfew on Tel Aviv. The bombing had an effect far beyond the damage it did by killing a large number of key British officials. It showed the Attlee government that Jews were now prepared to use any means and make any sacrifices to reach their objectives. It weakened the British determination to hang on to Palestine. They knew now that to do so, the cost would be tremendous, and they simply did not have the stomach to pay it

*   *   *

It took Abram a few months to adjust from being a warrior to being a civilian. Even though he identified himself totally with his fellow Jews, there was still something inside of him that made it difficult to feel strongly against the British. They were his comrades-in-arms throughout World War II. They liked him. They helped him, pushed for his promotions from an enlisted man to a major. He came to admire the English and their country. He was in a state of turmoil and was psychologically torn by conflicting emotions. In the British Army he was on top; he was a major. British soldiers saluted him when he passed them. Suddenly he didn't know what to do with himself. He had no place of his own, no money, nothing to do. He had to look for a job.

One day a man from a Tel Aviv bus co-op approached him. The co-op had 800 owner–partners. Many of them had served in Abram's unit during the war. He told Abram that they would like him to join. He could pay for his share from his earnings. At first he would be driving a bus, but was promised that if everything went well, he would be given the management of the bus repair shop. Abram accepted and became a bus driver. He found a job for Hy in an army workshop.

More World War II survivors were coming into Palestine in spite of British efforts to hold the Jewish immigration to a minimum. The new arrivals were different from the original Palestinian Jewish immigrants who were strong and dynamic. The new refugees, even though their hearts were in the right place, were still suffering from the trauma of their terrible experiences with the Nazis.

About the same time, a Haganah representative approached Abram. They wanted him to join the Palmach, the fighting arm of the Haganah. Unfortunately, a situation developed that weakened the potential strength of the Jewish armed forces. Ben-Gurion surrounded himself with military advisors who were bigshots in the Haganah and had political influence, but didn't have real military ability or leadership experience.

Many of them served at sub-officer level in the British Army during World War II.

When the Arabs attacked a few months later, Ben-Gurion's men were unable to cope with the situation. They were forced to turn to the former Jewish British Army officers for help in organization and training, but they still wanted to be bosses. This caused a lot of friction, and initially cost the Jews dearly.

Abram was getting sick to his stomach watching the new Jewish military commanders vying for Ben-Gurion's attention. It reminded him of the Jewish orthodox rabbi in Hrubieszow surrounded by his students, dancing around him as he walked down the street. Still he knew he had no choice. It was a matter of Jewish survival. He quit his job and joined the Palmach even though he had no respect for its leaders. Many former Jewish Brigade officers joined the Palmach as well.

In the meantime, events occurred that turned out to be decisive to Jews in Palestine and Europe. The King David bombing by the Irgun, which killed a large number of British subjects, was condemned as terrorism by many, including some Jewish leaders. But it did have a profound effect on the British government and the English people. The conservative opposition in Parliament had begun pressing for the end of the Mandate. Winston Churchill said, "If we cannot fulfill our promises to the Zionists, we should, without delay, place our Mandate for Palestine at the feet of the United Nations, and give due notice of our impending evacuation from that country." Churchill, even though he had been voted out of power, still carried a lot of weight. On February 18, 1947, the Attlee government made a statement to the effect that since they had no power to award the country to Jews or Arabs, they would submit the matter to the United Nations.

The Jewish leadership itself was divided as to how to handle the situation. Chaim Wiezman, who certainly was as instrumental in the creation of Israel as anybody else, spoke before the 22nd Jewish Congress in Basel, Switzerland, on December 16,

1946. He was old and almost blind, but he wanted to make sure
no major mistake was made that would affect the ultimate goal
of creating a Jewish State. He spoke against using terrorism as a
weapon. Even though the audience gave him a standing ova-
tion out of the respect they had for the great man, many disagreed with him. Certainly, looking back at all these events
from the perspective of history, there seems to be little doubt
that Lehi and Irgun acts, abhorrent as they were to all civilized
people, were probably decisive in at least getting the British to
withdraw sooner than anticipated, and thus perhaps, instrumental in changing the entire course of events.

As the British withdrawal appeared imminent, a war with
the Arabs became inevitable. The surrounding Arab states were
held back from intervention by the presence of the British
Army. They were now free to send in their well equipped
armies to help their brethren fight the Jews. The Jews knew that
faced with an imminent attack of the combined Arab armies,
their high spirit and willingness to die for their cause alone
would not be enough. They needed weapons, they needed
training, they needed money, and at least some moral support
from the rest of the world.

Abram was doing his best to train the Palmach members in
the art of using weapons and military tactics, but his heart was
heavy. As a former officer, he understood the tremendous odds
the Jews were facing and that it would take a near miracle to
save himself and the others from an Arab massacre. The Jewish
military force he was helping to create was unlike any other
army. There were no ranks. People with experience were just
telling other people what to do.

After the bombing of the King David Hotel, the British
Army — albeit unofficially — now completely turned against
the Jews. They enlisted Arab help and destroyed Ben Yehuda
Street in Jerusalem with explosives, causing about 200 casualties. With Arab help they blew up the Sochnut (Haganah political headquarters). Many top Jewish Haganah leaders were

killed or injured. All this happened without the British admitting any involvement. Abram, still conditioned by years of fighting side by side with many British soldiers and officers, became very upset by the British actions.

The Arabs, encouraged by the British, increased their own attacks on the Jews. They destroyed an entire medical convoy on the way to Mt. Scopus in Jerusalem, and killed seventy Jews, most of them doctors, nurses, and other medical personnel. The British just stood by and did nothing to help. The Arabs also destroyed a soap factory on the Tel Aviv-Sarafand Road and killed seven Jews there.

While the British were being evacuated to Gaza, Abram organized a camp for Jewish convoys on their way to Jerusalem. Abram's camp was only 200 feet from the road. One day a British soldier took aim at Abram and started shooting. The bullets hit the wall above the door and went over the heads of a number of Jews eating at a table. Other British soldiers from the same armored convoy killed two Jewish youths riding bicycles a little farther down the road.

It became clear to the Palestinian Jews that the Arabs' real aim was not just to have their Palestinian State, but to destroy all Jews. The Palmach, which until then was fighting only the Arabs, now joined the fight against the British as well. Bevin, the British Secretary of Labor, was an anti-Semite, and the British Army in Palestine reflected his feelings. They supported the Arabs in many ways, even gave them military equipment without receiving any payment. Even during their last weeks in Palestine, the British were still searching Jews for weapons. The Palmach, with its large number of members, now became the core of the Jewish Army that was in the process of being formed.

It was two million Palestinian Arabs, supported by all neighboring Arab states with their tens of millions of people and regular armies (including and well-trained Arab Legion commanded by Glubb Pasha and his English officers), pitted against 500,000 poorly armed Jewish men, women, and children. The only Arab voice of reason was that of the Jordanian King Abdullah (the grandfather of the now King Hussein). He believed that the problems between the Jews and the Arabs could be resolved peacefully. He was later assassinated by his fellow Arabs who wanted no compromise.

The British were hoping that now the Jews, seeing that they were in great danger, would beg them to stay to protect them. The Palmach gave them the answer. In a single night they blew up fourteen bridges to show the British how much the Jews wanted them out. In reprisal, the British caught fourteen Jews and shot them. One of the Jews executed by the British was a participant in the mission to blow up the bridges. Before the attack, Abram had given him his old British Army uniform which the man wore to help camouflage the action.

The Jews were outnumbered and they were barely defending themselves. The Arabs were primarily attacking Jewish convoys, but on a few occasions, they attacked Jewish settlements as well. They had some successes. They captured Gezer and a few other small settlements, killing hundreds of people and taking a number of prisoners.

Ben-Gurion and his political-military Palmach leaders still hadn't learned good military tactics. They tried to defend every town, every settlement, no matter how small, no matter how indefensible the position. Their tactics were stupid and cost many Jewish lives. Abram and other former British Army Jewish officers tried their best to explain this to the Palmach leaders, but to no avail.

～ 18 ～

UNITED NATIONS VOTES —
A DREAM COMES TRUE

The United Kingdom requested a special session of the General Assembly to consider the Palestinian matter. The British Foreign Office, full of intrigue and known for their anti-Zionist feelings, was secretly hoping for a deadlock in the United Nations (their proposal needed a two-thirds majority of the votes to pass). They thought that with the Soviet Bloc, the Arab countries, and their supporters among the smaller nations, they would be able to achieve that. This would let the British keep all options alive with regard to Palestine and gain valuable time for them. In the weeks preceding the vote, tensions in Palestine ran very high. In March an explosion at the Goldsmith Officers Club in Jerusalem killed eleven and injured many more people. Another round of executions and reprisals against the Jews followed.

Unexpectedly an event took place with the most significant political implications to the entire history of the Jewish struggle to create the State of Israel. The Soviet Foreign Minister, Andre Gromyko, made a statement during the debate outlining the Soviet position. He attacked the bankruptcy of the mandatory "system" of Palestine, and endorsed the "aspirations of the Jews to establish their own State." This was a bombshell, a real turn-around in Soviet policy. He would prefer a formation of a single state jointly ruled by Jews and Arabs, and if that turned out to be impossible, a partition of Palestine into an Arab State and a Jewish State.

What caused the Soviets to change their policy is a matter of speculation. Stalin's mind had always been difficult to read. His attitude toward Jews ranged from friendly to hostile depending on his mood, feelings of insecurity, etc. (The famous so-called "Doctors' Plot" shortly before Stalin's death almost certainly indicated a forthcoming purge of Jews, and perhaps, widespread Jewish persecutions. This, fortunately for the Soviet Jews, never materialized because of the sudden demise of the dictator.)

In Palestine tension between the British Army and the Jewish community continued to escalate. In July 1947, a British military unit captured three members of the Irgun and a British military court sentenced them to death. Irgun, in turn, captured two British sergeants and threatened to kill them if the British executed their fellow members. The three Irgunists were executed and a couple of days later the two British sergeants were found hanged. To make it worse, Irgun's people planted mines under the hanging bodies of the sergeants, and a number of British soldiers were badly injured when they came to cut the bodies down.

These events caused an outpouring of British wrath. In England there were anti-Semitic riots in a number of cities. The British troops in Tel Aviv fired on buses, smashed cafes, and committed all kinds of violence. A number of Jews lost their lives during these attacks.

In the meantime, more and more ships were on their way to Palestine loaded with Jewish survivors of World War II. The British were successful in intercepting many of those, mostly the larger ones, and interning their passengers on Cyprus, but some were getting through. The Jewish arrivals provided the locals with new manpower. Most of these, however, were still under the trauma of their war experiences, and even though many were ready to die for their new homeland, they could not be of much help until they received some minimum military training. The British internment of tens of thousands of survivors of the Holocaust was criticized in many countries, especially in the U.S.

One event in particular resulted in headlines everywhere and made the British look bad in the eyes of the world. It was the *Exodus* debacle. *Exodus* was an 1,800 ton American ship, previously known as the *President Warfield*. It carried 4,500 Jews — all survivors of concentration camps. Four British destroyers followed her. Before the *Exodus* reached the Palestinian shores, British troops stormed her, and attacked the mostly unarmed passengers who offered unexpected resistance. Three people on the *Exodus* were killed, dozens were wounded and were brought ashore at Haifa for hospitalization.

Thousands of people were on the seashore watching the *Exodus* come into port with the four British destroyers nearby. The scene created a worldwide sensation. In New York City 20,000 people marched in protest. The insensitive, anti-Semitic British Foreign Minister, Ernest Bevin, used the fact that *Exodus* left from the port of Marseilles to insist that its passengers return there instead of going to Cyprus.

The passengers were taken off the *Exodus,* transferred to several smaller British ships, and sent to Port de Bouc, France. A new crisis developed. The French government, unwilling to appear heartless to world opinion, offered the Jews asylum (which was not accepted), but refused to use force to take them ashore. The British Ambassador in Paris begged Bevin to withdraw the ship, but he refused and kept insisting that the French take them in, which they told him again they would not do by force. The British ships then proceeded to Luebeck, Germany, a port in the British occupation zone, and the survivors were taken to a Displaced Persons camp in Poppendorf. The *Exodus* incident captured the world's attention. Now sympathies shifted in favor of the Jews. Thus the Jews of *Exodus,* having gone through weeks of tension and frustration, were instrumental in shifting world opinion against the British Mandate.

On August 31, 1947, the United Nations team (UNSCOP), working on solutions for Palestine, completed its report. A seven to three majority recommended that Palestine be divided into Jewish and Arab States, keeping the holy places held under international control. The United States announced that it would strongly support the report. To become effective, the report required a two-thirds majority of the United Nations. The Arab League publicly condemned it.

The British government finally decided that it had enough of the Mandate. On October 17, Arthur Creech Jones, the Colonial Secretary, told the United Nations that Britain no longer wanted any responsibility for the partition and it would not even participate in its enforcement. They said that since they could not keep control, they would not help to enforce the Commission's recommendation. (Obviously, that would antagonize Egypt and Iraq, both of which were important to Great Britain.)

On November 29, 1947, the crucial vote took place in New York City during a meeting of the General Assembly of the United Nations. A great deal of pressure was put on President Truman not to vote for the partition, particularly by General George C. Marshall. Eddie Jacobson, Truman's former business partner, was persuaded by the indefatigable Chaim Weizmann to make an emotional appeal to the president to support the resolution. Jacobson begged Truman to see Weizmann, and a meeting was arranged. During this meeting, Weizmann poured his heart and soul out to Truman and succeeded in getting the wavering president to decide in favor of the partition. As Lord Passfield, no friend of Jews, said years before, "The whole thing is unfair because Jews have Weizmann and the Arabs do not." The Soviets played a crucial role as well. Their entire bloc voted for the partition.

Chaim Weizmann was in New York, sick, weak, and working feverishly, using the prestige it took a lifetime to build. He was in a frenzy, begging for a few additional votes. The Arab nations were using unrelenting pressure to defeat the resolution. Smaller countries were wavering back and forth under pressure from both sides. There were some last minute switches. Finally, the voting took place. Thirty-three countries voted for partition; thirteen, including eleven Muslim states, voted against it; and eleven abstained, including Great Britain.

In Palestine the United Nations vote was followed with great intensity and expectation by every Jew in Israel. They knew that the vote was by no means the end of their struggle. They fully expected an attack by all Arab States. They knew that the odds in that war would be all against them, but this vote was a moral victory, an acknowledgment that somehow, after all their sufferings, the majority of the world's nations were on their side. People everywhere — in the streets, in the kibbutzim, in offices — held their breath as nation after nation delivered its vote. When it became clear that the required two-thirds of the votes were assured, a tremendous cry of joy went out all over Palestine. People were singing and dancing in the streets, kissing and embracing each other.

The enemies of Zionism did not concede defeat easily. Before the British rule ended on April 23, 1948, a lot of maneuvering was taking place in and around the United Nations to reverse the decision on partition. President Truman was pressured to set up a temporary Trusteeship for Palestine, which would again delay and possibly kill the implementation of the partition. But Truman was not to be swayed this time. He told Judge Rosenman, one of his advisors, "I have Dr. Weizmann on my conscience." The U.S. Department of State, headed by General Marshall, was making a last ditch effort to kill the establishment of a Jewish State. Marshall even went as far as to warn Ben-Gurion against proclaiming a State.

But nothing would stop Ben-Gurion now. On May 14, he as

Prime Minister, issued a proclamation of the State of Israel. The British Mandate expired on May 15. Eleven minutes later, President Truman, de facto, recognized the State of Israel. He said, "The old Doctor (Weizmann) will believe me now." Ben-Gurion, Weizmann's rival for most of his life, sent him a message on behalf of the Government of Israel: "On the occasion of the establishment of the State of Israel, we send our greetings to you who have done more than any other living man toward its creation. Your stand and help have strengthened all of us. We look forward to the day when we shall see you as the head of the State established in peace."

On the date the Mandate expired, May 15, 1948, five surrounding Arab States attacked the one-day-old Jewish State. Egyptian war planes bombed Tel Aviv. Ben-Gurion spoke to his people from an air-raid shelter. The fight for survival of the new State and its people had begun.

~ 19 ~

FIVE ARAB STATES
ATTACK ISRAEL

The State of Israel as envisioned in the partition plan was a crazy mosaic with Arab and Jewish territories intersecting each other almost everywhere. Jerusalem was not alloted to the Jews. It was to be an international zone.

Fighting erupted everywhere; inside Palestine, Israelis were being attacked by the Palestinian Arabs; outside, armies of five Arab States were on the march to destroy the new State. Arabs had great expectations and could smell victory. They were encouraged by some of their successful forays against the Haganah in previous fighting, and now they felt that with all the Arab armies converging on Israel, they would soon bury the Jews.

The British Chiefs of Staff, still upset about all the trouble they had with the Palestinian Jews, predicted to their government, "The Arabs will throw the Jews into the sea." The Arabs, in a meeting in Damascus in April 1947, developed a plan on how to quickly destroy the new Jewish State. Syrian and Lebanese armies would come in from the north and occupy Tiberias, Safed, and Nazareth. The British-trained and British-commanded Arab Legion, supported by the Iraqi army would move west and occupy Haifa. The Egyptians would advance from the south on Tel Aviv. The Jordanian King Abdullah was to be Commander-in-Chief of all Arab armies.

However, in practice, old Arab enmities and jealousies came to the fore. There was no coordinated attack; instead, it became a piece-meal operation. The Syrians attacked the Jordan Valley and captured a small town, Zemah. On May 20 they attacked the large settlement of Degania, defended, among others, by Moshe Dayan. The seventy or eighty Jewish defenders used Molotov cocktails against the Syrian tanks whose occupants didn't know how to deal with these weapons and retreated. (Today one of those tanks is on display in Degania.) The news about this victory spread among the Jewish fighters everywhere and lifted their spirits tremendously.

The Lebanese army made a halfhearted attempt to enter northern Galilee, but after the Jews counterattacked, part of its forces withdrew back into Lebanon. A few Lebanese units penetrated into central Galilee where they were joined by local Arab units. Many of the Lebanese were Christian, and their hearts were not really in the war. Troops from Iraq, which didn't have a common border with Israel, were called the "Liberation Army" and were driven off the Jewish settlement of Gesher. They briefly captured the settlement of Geulim, but were thrown back by Jewish units which proceeded to chase them and laid siege to the Arab town of Jenin. That pretty much ended the Iraqi army's offensive operations in the war.

The largest Arab forces came in from Egypt. They were driving towards Tel Aviv. A small Jewish settlement named Yad Mordechai, after the hero of the Warsaw uprising against the Nazis, Mordechai Anielewich, held off superior Egyptian forces of one armored tank battalion, an artillery regiment, and two infantry battalions for five days, and was finally evacuated on May 24. Other Egyptian units captured a small settlement of Nizana. There an incident took place that increased the determination of the embattled Jews. The Egyptians lined up a number of Jews in the center of town and an Egyptian officer asked who was the senior among them. The man stepped out and the officer shot him. A Jewish girl, standing next in line, pulled out a gun and killed the officer. The Egyptian soldiers then shot and killed her. The Egyptian units proceeded north and arrived at a small kibbutz, Negba. The defenders of Negba, which numbered less than 100, put up a heroic stand. There were many people from Hrubieszow among the defenders. Egyptian forces equipped with tanks and artillery attacked for three days, but to no avail. They went around Negba and proceeded north, but were soon stopped by a unit of the Palmach.

The unexpected strong Jewish resistance against Egyptian forces, which were vastly superior in numbers and equipment, shocked the Egyptian soldiers and their officers. They expected an easy ride to Tel Aviv, but instead, encountered a small but determined enemy who inflicted large casualties on them. The Israelis were finally able to buy four Messerschmitt fighter planes and these became very helpful in stemming the Egyptian advance. The invaders, with their spirit and confidence greatly diminished, were content to remain in their positions for the time being.

The Israelis were very worried about the Jordanians with their Arab Legion. Now part of the Transjordanian Army, the Legion, which for years was trained and equipped by the British, was commanded by a top British Army officer with an adopted name, Glubb Pasha. And indeed, it was there, on the Jerusalem front, where the Jews suffered their greatest losses.

When the war against the newly born State broke out, Jews had only a smattering of weapons. Now, with the recognition of Israel, the procurement of weapons was legal, and the Haganah agents were feverishly at work buying weapons wherever they could get their hands on them, and shipping them to Israel. Another problem for the defenders was a lack of real military organization. Israel's army was composed of loosely knit units that were sent to places where the greatest dangers existed. It was a strange war, without a real contiguous front.

The Arab Legion attacked the Jewish sector of Jerusalem's New City, but were repulsed. They then switched the attack to the Jewish sector of the Old City, with mostly religious Jews who were uninterested in Zionism. On the morning of May 28, a delegation of rabbis went to the Jordanian command and received a promise by the Legion officers not to harm the Jewish population. The small Israeli garrison surrendered, and the Arabs were in control of Old Jerusalem. However, the defenders of the New City, mainly the Palmach units, continued to hold off all Arab Legion attacks. The Arabs succeeded in surrounding it. They were in control of Latrun, a fortress in the Valley of Ayalon, blocking the main supply road to Jerusalem from Tel Aviv.

Since Abram had a lot of experience in motorized transport during World War II, he became one of the leaders of the Central Transportation Command. The head of this command was Buganov, who was also a former British Army officer. Their job was the organization of supplies of war materiels and weapons, and the distribution of those to the fighting units. Abram was given the task of setting up twenty-one workshops all over Israel.

One of the memorable incidents in Abram's life took place toward the end of May. Brigadier Marcus was an American Jew. He distinguished himself in the American Army during World War II and was a great supporter of Israel. He raised money and helped to buy weapons for the Israeli soldiers. He came to Israel and was well-intentioned, but somewhat of a loose cannon, and a heavy drinker. For a while he stayed in the same tent with Abram. He was exhorting the Jews to fight; even with stones if no other weapons were available. Unfortunately, he died in a tragic accident. He was in an army camp near Abugosh and left his tent one night to urinate. It was chilly, so he threw a white blanket over his shoulders. A Jewish guard mistook him for an Arab and shot him to death.

The situation of the defenders of the New City of Jerusalem became desperate. Surrounded on all sides, they were running out of food and military supplies. Ben-Gurion, with no military experience, ordered an attack on Arab-held Latrun, which was blocking the road. Abram was near the unit which was set to attack the fortress, defended by the Arab Legion with its artillery and British officers. Abram could tell that the unit, consisting of 1,800 men was poorly trained and equipped to attack. Many of them were survivors of the Holocaust who were high on enthusiasm but had practically no military training. Shlomo Shamir was in charge. Abram told Shamir that it would be foolish to attack Latrun with his unit, but if it was critically important, at least the attack should take place at night.

It was 4 A.M. and Ben-Gurion was on the phone with Shamir insisting the attack be carried out. During the conversation, Abram kept asking Shamir to tell Be- Gurion that it would be suicidal. Ben-Gurion insisted. Shamir did not want to disobey direct orders from Ben-Gurion, so the attack took place. Abram watched the attackers advance uphill against withering Jordanian fire. Hundreds of dead and wounded were on the hill leading to the fortress, but this did not deter the others. A few got close to the police station, but were driven back. This foolish attack caused the greatest Jewish losses of the War of Independence. Many hundreds were killed and hundreds more wounded. Jerusalem was still surrounded, its inhabitants and soldiers near starvation.

~ 20 ~

THE BURMA ROAD —
FIGHTING BEN-GURION

On September 1, 1948, Abram was informed at the Yaffa Head-quarters that Ben-Gurion wanted to see him at 2 P.M. at his headquarters in the Red House, which was on the Mediter-ranean seashore. Abram arrived at the exact hour without hav-ing the slightest idea what this was all about. Ben-Gurion was asleep. His wife, Pola, was watching over him. Abram told Pola that he was called in for an appointment with her husband. She told Abram that Ben-Gurion was very tired, needed some rest, and asked if he would please wait.

A half hour later Ben-Gurion was up. He said, "Silberstein, come; we must talk." He told Abram that he had heard about him and his experiences in the British Army, especially in the commandos, and that he was the right man for a job Ben-Gurion had in mind. He explained because of the failure to re-capture Latrun, the road to Jerusalem was closed, and that the Jewish population there was starving. There was a desperate need for an alternative road. Amos Horev, accompanied by two men, was able to pass through the mountains on foot, circling around Arab-held positions. They believed that there was a chance to establish a secret supply route to Jerusalem through the mountains, but felt that this should be confirmed by a transport expert.

Ben-Gurion asked, "Could you do the job?" Abram said, "Give me twenty-four hours to do some reconnaissance." After leaving Ben-Gurion, he met with Amos Horev and got from him a number of details marked on a map, and other pertinent information.

Abram took a jeep, two experienced men, and several buckets of whitewash and brushes. Armed with Tommy guns, they left at night. When they got to the hills, Abram started crawling in front of the jeep, whitewashing marks on the rocks in places where he thought it was possible for jeeps to pass. The jeep followed him slowly. At one point they almost stepped onto a platoon of Palmach soldiers that was hiding, ready to ambush any Arab units that would pass by. They told Abram, "We heard you whisper in Hebrew to each other, and that saved your lives."

It took them about two hours to cross over the steep hills. They returned to Ben-Gurion's headquarters using the same passage. Abram told Ben-Gurion, "Give me jeeps and I'll do the job."

Abram personally picked out experienced drivers for the twelve jeeps assigned for the mission. They loaded each jeep with only 2½ sacks of flour. They were afraid to put in more weight because each jeep carried a driver and an armed guard and had to climb extremely steep, rocky hills. They drove with the windshields down. Driving over the rocks caused the jeep mufflers to lose their effectiveness. The jeeps were making a lot of noise, and the Arab snipers started firing at the convoy. Luckily, because of the noise, the Arabs may have thought that Abram's convoy included tanks, so they refrained from a direct attack.

During the fourth supply trip, two of Abram's men were killed by Arab bullets, and a jeep became incapacitated. They decided to burn it. The stress from driving night after night under extremely difficult conditions caused great strain to Abram's eyes. Upon his arrival back to Bilu, he started to undress when a messenger came in and told him that Ben-Gurion was waiting for him at Hulda. As Abram was putting on his battle dress, one of his men gave him a copy of the evening paper, *Maariv*. There was a huge headline across the front page, "The Road To Jerusalem Is Now Open." In the article there was an exact description of Abram's group's "modus operandi."

On his way to Hulda, Abram could hardly contain his fury. He was ushered immediately into Ben-Gurion's room. When Ben-Gurion spotted him, he asked all the others to leave. He said he wanted to talk to Abram in private. He wanted to know the exact amount of flour Abram and his men were able to get through to Jerusalem. When Abram gave him the information, Ben-Gurion snapped sharply, "That's not enough. I am holding you responsible for the fall of Jerusalem."

Abram had had enough. He threw the *Maariv* newspaper on the table and said, "You are killing the whole project by disclosing to the Arabs our way of operation. Why did you have to do it?" Ben-Gurion shouted, "Remember, you are only a soldier on the front line. Leave the politics to me." Abram answered, "Yes, Sir, but you cannot win a war with dead soldiers." Then he really opened up. He said, "Sir, there are too many unpardonable mistakes made. The lesson of Latrun shouldn't be forgotten. During the Latrun battle, I was standing next to Shamir at his headquarters when you, Sir, were calling every ten minutes urging him to attack, although it was already daylight. I was the one who told him to disobey your order, unfortunately to no avail."

Ben-Gurion lowered his head, hit it with both hands, and sat down with his head still down. He was breathing heavily, thick veins visibly pulsating on his neck. Abram got very scared. He thought that Ben-Gurion was having a heart attack. Ben-Gurion stayed in that position for a long time, perhaps ten minutes. Not a single word was uttered. Suddenly, as if nothing had happened between them, he lifted his head and said, "All right, what kind of help do you need?"

Abram said, "Sir, mules and more mules. A jeep can carry only 2½ sacks of flour through the mountains, while a mule can easily carry six." "Where can I get those mules?" Ben-Gurion asked. "Cyprus, Sir. I saw them used in an operation in Italy when I was with the VIIIth Army," answered Abram. Somewhat shakily Ben-Gurion said, "I will get them for you." Abram left the room. In just a couple of days Abram was supplied with a couple dozen of mules. Mark, a Greek officer whom Abram knew from the campaign in Italy, was taking care of the animals. Using mules, Abram was able to supply more flour and other necessities to the beleaguered Jerusalem.

In the meantime the Jewish Army had successfully completed Operation Nachshon, which resulted in chasing the Arabs out of their positions in the mountains. Abram, now less concerned about being ambushed by the Arabs, widened the "Burma Road" with the help of a few bulldozers, and supplying Jerusalem became much easier. The Arabs tried to attack the new road from time to time, but were unable to do much damage as their big guns in Latrun were too far away. Even today the "Burma Road" serves as a secondary road from Tel Aviv to Jerusalem.

The following is a translation from Ben-Gurion's diary in *The War of Independence*. The date is September 6, 1948, Wednesday (page 208)

Abraham Silberstein, the second in command to Shemer, arrived at four o'clock in the morning. He reported that the porters came back late at three o'clock in the morning; they were tired.

He said that the jeeps went up passing through the Arab positions with the food. The mules were held up for five hours as the passage was blocked by a broken down jeep between the rocks. One hundred and fifty men were left in Beit Susin; an additional 150 men remained in the base of Bilu. It is believed that the men and mules will be able to go up.

The new, wider road is being constructed, although it winds within the range of Arabic fire.

The attack that took place that night wasn't the one planned by Yadin, and he doesn't understand why Stone and Ygal Alon altered it.

It is clear from Ygal's conversation with the H.Q. that no action towards Latrun will be taken that night, probably due to shortage of ammunition. Stone is asking for supporting weapons. They will act tomorrow. According to Silberstein, food will be carried again tonight to Jerusalem by jeeps, mules and men.

At six-thirty I return to Ramat Gan.*

Abram received new orders from the Army. The Palmach was holding a number of positions on the Egyptian front, but there was no reliable way to supply them. They flew Abram to the southern front and asked him to organize transportation to the Palmach units all over the Negev Desert. Abram went back, and using two small planes, returned to the Negev with twenty mechanics. Because Egyptian planes were bombing Jewish positions, Abram and his men built an underground storage facility. To his delight, he found out that the Italian arms he had stolen from the British Army during World War II and sent to Palestine were being used by Jewish soldiers on all fronts. The workshops became operational in short order, and they started

---

*For whatever reason, Ben-Gurion's diary does not nearly tell the whole story of his meetings with Abram.

supplying the army units in the Negev Desert using Dakota planes. The Israelis now felt more confident about the outcome of the war.

Before the attack by the five Arab States had begun, many Jews, particularly older people, were in mortal fear of the future. They did not know that the invading Arab armies had many inherent weaknesses. Now, even though they had succeeded in containing the Arab forces, the Jews knew that the situation was still frought with danger. The Israeli Army was really a conglomeration of loosely connected units. Several hundred volunteers, including some pilots (almost all Jewish) came from the U.S., England, France, South Africa, and other countries. Some of them had military experience and that was helpful. These volunteers lifted the Israelis' spirits. It felt good to know that they had the support of Jews all over the world. The Army was able to procure about fifty military aircraft, mostly fighters, and a number of Egyptian bombers were shot down.

After the fighting resumed, the Israelis counterattacked in several areas. Yadim was in charge of the Army; Dayan became one of his key generals. Joseph Tabenkin led a well-organized Palmach attack on the Latrun fortress. This time the Jews had better weapons, and their soldiers were well-trained. Arab resistance had weakened under a withering assault and soon an Israeli flag flew high over the area.

A number of the English soldiers deserted during their Army's withdrawal from Palestine, and joined the Arab Legion to fight the Jews. Abram was near a wireless station when he overheard an English sergeant on the radio, "You Jewish bastards. You won't pass this time (meaning Latrun)." Abram told the sergeant that he had been a British Army major and added, "We will fuck your bloody asses." At first the sergeant apparently didn't believe Abram. He said, "You are not a major." Abram replied, "I will give you my serial number, you bastard."

Under Jewish pressure, the Egyptian Army started to retreat from the positions they occupied during their initial drive into Palestine. Abram and his soldiers entered Majdal, a village in the Negev. They were proceeding very slowly because they were not sure whether all the Egyptians had actually left Majdal. As they were walking down a street with their guns at the ready, a door opened; a woman came out and asked, "Sie reden Yiddish?" (Do you speak Yiddish?) It turned out that she was a prostitute from Beirut who chose to settle in Majdal. She assured them that the Egyptians had left some time before, and that there was no danger.

Before the Jews gained the upper hand in the war, events on the political front were in a turmoil. On May 29, 1949, the Security Council of the United Nations adopted a resolution which contained, besides a call for a cease-fire, a provision prohibiting the importation of arms to Palestine or the Arab states. The actual cease-fire did not, in reality, take place until June 11. At the time, the Jews did not fully realize how weak the Arab armies were and greeted the event with joy. They needed time to organize their forces, and to procure more weapons.

At this decisive moment, an incident took place which caused a great rift among the Jews and did a lot of damage to their cause. On May 28, Ben-Gurion issued an order officially creating the Israeli Defense Forces. The order prohibited existence of any independent Jewish armed units. However, the Irgun, which at one time was a small terrorist organization, had grown substantially in numbers and strength, and continued to operate independently. The French government decided to provide arms for the Irgun. They shipped a large quantity of weapons on a ship named *Altalena,* which was Vladimir Zabotinsky's pen name. They promised even more supplies for the Irgun. The sailing of *Altalena* was widely publicized. In addition to arms, *Altalena* carried a number of Irgun volunteers, mostly Jewish.

Ben-Gurion was now caught in a dilemma. The Jews needed the arms badly. On the other hand, this was a flagrant violation of the Security Council's resolution, and more importantly, it would considerably strengthen the Irgun, which Ben-Gurion knew he could not really control. It was a heartbreaking decision, but Ben-Gurion issued the orders to set *Altalena* on fire on the beach of Tel Aviv. The order was carried out by the Haganah. In the ensuing fighting, fifteen men were killed, mostly members of the Irgun.

Menachem Begin, an Irgun leader, was on board the *Altalena*. He knew that a war among Jews would have catastrophic consequences for the newly created State. To his credit, he broadcast a statement over the Irgun underground transmitter. He said, in effect, that from that point on, the Irgun would pursue only political activities within the State of Israel itself, but that it would continue military actions in territories alloted to the Arabs. Ben-Gurion accepted this solution to avoid any extended fighting among Jews. However, even today, bitter memories of the *Altalena* events still linger on.

The truce that was called for by the Security Council on May 29 didn't take effect until June 11. It gave each side time to regroup and re-supply its forces. The United Nations appointed the Swedish Count Bernadotte as the Palestine mediator, and Ralph Bunche, the American diplomat, as his deputy. Perhaps because of his family background, the Count found some of the Arab aristocratic leaders easier to deal with than the brash and aggressive Israelis. He and Bunche developed a plan that was presented to all parties on June 27. The plan called for Jordan to retain the West Bank; the Palestinian Arabs to have the Negev; and the Jews to hold a narrow corridor along the Mediterranean Sea and parts of Galilee. It also left the question of future Jewish immigration subject to United Nations approval. All Arab refugees (500,000 of them left their homes during the fighting) were to return to their homes, mostly in territories now alloted to Israel. All parties rejected

Bunche's proposal out of hand. The Jews did it because the territory alloted to them was extremely limited, and even their sovereignty was not fully recognized under the plan.

The Arabs still didn't understand, or want to admit to themselves, the obvious weakness they showed during the fighting. Only King Abdullah was realistic enough to see the situation clearly. Other Arabs, particularly the heads of states that invaded Israel, kept promising quick victories and the destruction of the new Jewish State, and were caught up in their own lies. They were not willing to accept their defeats and kept boasting to their peoples about fictitious victories. Jews, even though still traumatized by the initial fear of five states invading their tiny new country, were now confident and getting stronger each day.

On July 9 fighting broke out in the Negev, but the Arabs failed in all their attacks. The Israelis succeeded in widening the corridor to Jerusalem. They captured the Arab towns of Lydda and Ramle in lower Galilee. Arabs spread news of Jewish atrocities committed on Arab civilians, and tens of thousands of Arabs again fled their homes. In actuality, the Jews didn't harm the Arab civilians, although they did not discourage them from leaving either. Deir Yassin was an exception where the Irgun fighters killed a number of Arab civilians. The other rumors of mass killings were spread by Arab propagandists and caused new waves of refugees to leave their homes. Most of them fled to Gaza and the West Bank held by Jordanian troops.

An Interesting Wartime Vignette

In 1946 in Belgium while we were in the midst of moving the concentration camp survivors to Marseilles, I happened to be invited to visit a Jewish family in Brussels. The family, luckily, survived the Holocaust in hiding, and now kept an open house for the Jewish Brigade.

That evening there were a few youngsters in the room, and drinks were served. A 16-year-old girl, a friend of the family, was sitting in a corner crying. I started a conversation. She told me that she had lost her entire family, and she was all alone.

I asked her if she would be willing to take a chance and go to Palestine. She told me she would if it could be arranged. I took her address, and told her to stay at home the following morning, and two of my sergeants would pick her up at ten o'clock.

Two years later, in 1948, we were fighting the Egyptian Army in the Negev which was cut off completely in the North. I was dropped there by plane in an effort to help solve a transportation problem.

I made my base in kibbutz Ruhama. One morning we were told that the Egyptians were attacking the outpost of kibbutz Rvivim. We assembled fifteen men with rifles and went to Rvivim in two small trucks. When we finally reached the place, there was no fighting, no shooting. An Egyptian armored half-truck was burning right in front of the barbed wire fence, and a few corpses were strewn around it. Behind the fence there was only one little old stone wall relic and a multitude of trenches in the deep sand. We didn't dare to come close as there were mines around.

A sunburned girl of about 18, in shorts with a rifle across her hips came out to us from the trenches. Speaking Hebrew with a strong French accent, she told us how they had beaten off the Egyptian attack. I suddenly realized that this was the girl from Brussels that I put on the convoy to Palestine. Now she was defending Israel. It was a moving moment, and it was difficult to hold back my tears. Abram Silberstein

The fighting in this round was short-lived. The Arabs now were faced with the bitter truth that they had lost the war. The hostilities by and large ended about July 17, although some localized fighting took place here and there, particularly in divided Jerusalem.

Another event now took place which was sad and unfortunate for the Jewish image of an underdog fighting against all odds. On September 17, 1948, three members of the Lehi assassinated Count Bernadotte in Jerusalem. There was worldwide criticism of the murder of this dedicated man. Ben-Gurion used this occasion to get rid of his enemies. He disbanded the Irgun and arrested a number of the Lehi adherents. For the first time, he had complete control of the Jewish forces.

Israel, now feeling its oats, decided to press the military advantage they had obtained during the fighting. Ben-Gurion and his ministers were considering taking control of both the West Bank and the Negev. In the end they decided that it might be too difficult to obtain both objectives and chose to attack the Egyptians in the Negev. Jewish forces attacked in September and again in December, driving the Egyptians completely out of the Negev Desert. They even pushed into the Sinai, an undisputed Egyptian territory.

Unexpectedly, Israel's old enemy, the British Foreign Minister Bevin, interceded again in the conflict. Britain offered to invoke the Anglo-Egyptian Treaty of 1936 in defense of Egypt. He sent R.A.F. planes on reconnaissance missions over Israeli-held territory. On January 7, 1949, Israeli forces shot down five of these planes. As ridiculous as it might appear, it looked as if Great Britain and Israel might actually blunder into a war. Fortunately, this time it was the Egyptians who saved the situation. They knew now that they could not defeat the Israelis, and perhaps didn't want to get involved more closely with Great Britain. It finally became clear to all the Arab states that they were badly beaten.

Negotiations followed which resulted in an armistice, which Egypt signed on February 24, 1949; Lebanon on March 23; Jordan on April 3, and Syria on July 20. Iraq, which did not have a common border with Israel, did not sign. It made no difference in the overall situation.

～ 21 ～

THE FRUITS OF VICTORY

The war had broad and long-term repercussions for the Arabs. Somebody had to be blamed for the Arab defeat. Egypt's Premier Nokrashy was assassinated in December of 1948. In Syria, there were three coups in 1949 alone. Jordan's King Abdullah was assassinated by the Jerusalem muftis' men on July 20, 1951. His grandson, Hussein, later became King of Jordan, continuing the Hashemite dynasty. For over thirty years he ruled and is still ruling his kingdom. Generally considered a moderate he, for a short while, sided with Saddam Hussein of Iraq against the U.S. during the Gulf War. This mistake temporarily cost him a loss of prestige in the U.S.

For Israel's Jews victory seemed miraculous. It was a dream come true, but it was hard to absorb it and believe it. After so many years of working, fighting, dreaming, hoping, and after all the British betrayals and Arab hatred, they finally had a home. They were walking tall in the streets of Tel Aviv, in the villages, and in the kibbutzim. Outnumbered, they had been able to look the invading Arab armies in the eye and defeat them decisively. Jews all over the world were proud of their sisters and brothers. People everywhere who often considered Jews weak and cowardly gained new respect for them.

The war was over, but the Jews didn't have much time to celebrate their victory. Tens of thousands of survivors were coming in from internment camps on Cyprus and from all over Europe. Relative to Israel's population of just a little over half a million people, this was a huge number to absorb, house, feed, and train for new jobs.

Israel's first election of the Knesset members, the new parliament, was held in January 1949. Ben-Gurion and his party, Mapay, won and continued as the largest force in Israel's politics for many years. Menachem Begin's Herut, a conservative party, was to become the main opposition.

Ben-Gurion invited Chaim Weizmann to return as president to the country he loved so much. Weizmann accepted. However, it soon became apparent that the office of the presidency didn't carry much power. Weizmann was disappointed, but there wasn't much he could do. Ben-Gurion again showed his insensitivity and tendency to be vindictive when he refused to add Weizmann's name to the list of signatures of Israel's Declaration of Independence.

Israelis were still haunted by the memories of the Holocaust. They felt very insecure in a world that permitted this atrocity to take place, and knew that without a strong army, their survival would be threatened. All political parties were in agreement on that point, and the new state devoted much energy and gave top priority to creating one of the world's finest, best-equipped, and best-trained armies.

The Israeli Army's leaders knew of Abram's role in World War II and his experience in motorized transport and put him in charge of all military workshops in Israel. Yadim, the head of the army, and Sapir called Abram in for a number of meetings. The army had only commercial trucks and needed to replace them with military ones. They started negotiations with the U.S. government, but for political reasons, the U.S. refused to sell military trucks to Israel. After numerous meetings and pressure from American Jewish leaders, the U.S. finally agreed to sell 3,000 farm trucks to Israel.

Abram was given the task of converting these trucks into military ones. He suggested that they be shipped in parts rather than fully assembled in order to save money in American labor and freight. He was told that the Israeli Army didn't want to be in the truck assembly business, and a suggestion was made that Abram become a contractor and do the assembly on his own. Abram started laughing. He said, "Do you want to make me a rich man?" The Army procurement officers insisted that Abram handle the conversion on his own, but wanted a guarantee of performance. Abram had no money, so they told him that since the business would be lucrative, he should have no trouble getting partners for this venture. He took in two partners with money, and became a businessman.

The Army offered Abram the use of army sheds for the truck assembly. Abram knew that for a big job like this, he needed good mechanics. He went to a refugee camp near Haifa and asked for people experienced in sheet metal, carpentry, painting, etc. He took 150 craftsmen with him out of the camps. Many were elderly and spoke a multitude of languages. Abram assured them, "Don't worry, we will teach you." They assembled 3,000 trucks in fifteen months, and reinforced them to meet the army requirements. He and his partners made money on this project. Abram used this money to build an apartment for himself. Later he, with Hy's help, added a second story for Hy to live in. Abram and other former army officers received parcels of free land in recognition of their services. This land was originally expropriated by the English Mandate government from German colonists.

After the work on the 3,000 trucks was done, a top Army official called Abram in to his office. He said, "You did such a good job with the trucks, we want you now to work for the army and build the largest repair shop for our military."

Abram worked out plans for the repair shop, and hired the workers to build it. He trained 200 people and supervised their work. He was being paid a very good salary and continued to manage the shop from 1951 until 1963.

In the meantime new events were taking place which shaped the future of Israel. Jews in North Africa and in the Middle East became the subject of persecution in many of the countries where they had lived for centuries. All through Jewish history, beginning in 732 B.C. when Jewish slaves were sent to Assyria, Babylon, and Egypt, Palestine and its Jewish inhabitants were victims of invasions and occupation by these countries, as well as by the Romans and the Turks. For eight centuries they were forced to flee their homes or be taken into slavery. Many of them and their descendants made their new homes in North African Mediterranean countries, as well as Syria, Persia, Turkey and the Arab Peninsula. They remained there for more than 2,000 years and they lived in relative peace. They were called the Sephardim (as opposed to the Ashkenazim who immigrated from Europe).

When the persecutions became prevalent after the War of Independence, 600,000 of the Sephardic Jews escaped to Israel. They were very different from the Ashkenazim. Their skin was darker, and they tended to be less aggressive. In the beginning, Israel was to them a place of refuge, unlike what it was for the Ashkenazim who fought so hard, suffered so much, and were so proud of their new country. Most of the newcomers had to learn Hebrew as well as the skills of a modern society. Frictions developed between the two groups. The job of absorbing the new immigrants was immense. New housing had to be built for them. Just imagine, proportionately this was the equivalent of the U.S. absorbing 200 million new immigrants in a few short years.

The Ashkenazim looked down on the Sephardim. They called them "blacks." They worried that they would cause a deterioration in Israel's quality of life. To its credit, the Ben-Gurion government showed no hesitation. The new Jewish State would take in any Jews from anywhere, no matter what the cost. Slowly the Sephardim took root in their new country. They appreciated the freedom, the lack of persecution, the opportunities. In time the two groups began to intermarry and became more homogenous. Today, even though there are still some frictions, by and large, the Sephardic Jews are an integral part of the Israeli society.

One day, when Abram was in his office at the workshops, Ben-Gurion came to pay him a visit. He was much different from the man with whom Abram had the confrontation during the war. He took some photos of Abram and then told him he wanted him to do two things. First, he asked Abram to change his name to a Hebrew one, which many Jews were doing at the time. Secondly, he wanted him to go to Germany to procure certain materials for the army which were difficult to obtain elsewhere. Abram said to Ben-Gurion, "Sir, with all due respect, I cannot do these two things. I shall never change my name out of respect for my father. Secondly, I cannot go to Germany. I will not be able to bring myself to sit at the same table with the Germans." Ben-Gurion replied, "Well, I can see your point." As he was walking out, he asked, "Tell me, which kibbutz do you belong to?" Abram told him that he didn't belong to any, but he happened to live not far from Ben-Gurion.

In 1954 Ben-Gurion asked that Abram be sent to the U.S. to learn the latest technology of running a truck workshop. First, Abram went to the International Center "Point 4" in Washington, D.C. to find out what America was all about. From there he went to Atlanta where he spent five months learning how the Atlanta Transit System ran. He came to a conclusion that the weather conditions in Atlanta were different from those in Israel, and therefore, many of the methods were not applicable to Israel. He decided to go to Tucson where the desert conditions were similar to those in most of Israel. He spent about six weeks in Tucson and travelled through the Yuma Desert to California.

From there he went to Detroit where he was the guest of the Chrysler Corporation for a couple of months. The most important thing he observed was that in the U.S., individual shops did not try to repair engines. These were shipped to a central repair center that specialized in repairing engines of all kinds. He came back to Israel and continued to run the workshop, applying some of the technologies he had learned in the U.S.

Unexpectedly, new hostilities broke out. This time it was with Egypt alone. The Egyptian leader, Gamal Abdal Nasser, became, after Egypt's takeover of the Suez Canal, a hero not only to the Egyptians, but to Arabs everywhere. He was electrifying his audiences with his nationalistic pan-Arabic speeches. He was making anti-Israeli statements and his government-controlled radio was spewing anti-Semitic propaganda. He was permitting the "Fedayeem" to raid Jewish settlements, which was not allowed under the armistice agreement. It all amounted to guerilla warfare against Israel. Ben-Gurion ordered a massive raid led by Ariel Sharon against Egyptian installations in Gaza. Thirty-six Egyptian soldiers were killed. This was a great humiliation for Nasser who was not in a position to go to war with Israel.

However, Nasser's nationalism became a threat to the British as well. They felt that he might endanger the safety of the Suez Canal, which was essential to Great Britain's access to the Middle East and particularly to the British Empire's crown jewel, India. Anthony Eden, who was then the British Prime Minister, wanted to get rid of Nasser. The French were also worried about Nasser. His continuous nationalistic Arab propaganda was stirring up unrest in Algeria, a key French possession in North Africa.

The British leaders came up with what they thought was a clever idea. Neither they nor the French wanted to antagonize the Arab world by declaring war against Egypt, so they cooked up a scheme. Israel, which was under continuous pressure from Nasser, would attack Egypt, and Great Britain and France would "intervene," to separate the fighting armies and to protect the Suez Canal. They hoped that this would topple Nasser without arousing the wrath of the Arab world.

Israeli leaders were flattered and excited by the prospect of becoming the Great Powers' partner in this adventure. Ben-Gurion and his military staff knew that war against Egypt was inevitable. They didn't want to give Nasser time to teach his soldiers how to use all the weapons he was acquiring from Czechoslovakia and other countries. The French now were sending weapons to Israel, and Jewish military leaders believed that they could defeat Egypt. Besides, why fight a war alone in the future with a stronger Egypt, when they could fight it now with the British and French as their partners in arms?

On October 29, 1956, the Israelis dropped parachute troops inside Sinai about 30 miles from the Suez Canal. In eight days, led by Moshe Dayan, Israeli soldiers routed the Egyptian Army and threw it out from all of Sinai including Sharm El Sheik, where Egyptian artillery had closed all Israeli shipping to the Gulf of Aqaba. Britain and France continued their charade by issuing a phony ultimatum to both Egypt and Israel. No one was fooled. The whole world knew what was going on. The British and French forces finally landed on November 6, but tremendous international pressure caused the entire venture to fail. The United Nations condemned the attack. President Eisenhower let Britain and France know how unhappy he was with them. Even more importantly, the Soviets threatened to intervene militarily.

Israeli leaders took the Soviet threat seriously. Ben-Gurion made a hollow "victory speech." He declared that the Armistice with Egypt was dead; dismissed the need for a United Nations force to be stationed between Egypt and Israel; and wanted his listeners to believe that Israel defeated France and England as well. Later that day, the General Assembly of the United Nations voted by a margin of 65 to 1 calling on Israel to withdraw. The only vote cast for Israel was by Israel itself. The United States put tremendous pressure on Ben-Gurion to withdraw immediately, threatening to cancel all aid, both government and private, for Israel. Even the President of the World Zionist Organization, Nahum Goldman, told the Israelis that American Jews would not support the continuation of the Sinai venture. Ben-Gurion, himself, later admitted that he must have been "drunk with victory to make the 'victory speech.'"

The Israeli government approved, on November 8, the withdrawal of its forces from the Sinai. However, the Sinai adventure had some positive effects as well. The Israeli Army demonstrated to the world, and particularly to the Arabs, that it now had developed into a powerful, modern, combat force to be reckoned with, and it injected new confidence and pride among the Israeli people in themselves and its army.

Before the actual withdrawal, Abram was given orders by the army to dismantle a number of Egyptian refineries on the Suez Canal. He and his team took three days to do the job, and brought home with them hundreds of refinery parts, mostly pipes and pumping equipment.

Abram's old army buddy, Tiber, who served in the British Army as a sergeant in Abram's unit, and who during the war brought to Abram the suitcase full of gold bars to help obtain the Italian weapons stored in Alexandria, approached Abram and offered him an important position in his Zion Insurance Company. Zion Insurance had several hundred employees. Abram would advise the company executives on the merits of issuing large insurance policies to potential customers and would have the final word in approving large settlements. The position called for someone with great integrity and Tiber knew that Abram was his man. After all, he was there when Abram brought the weapons from Alexandria without using any of the gold he was given to accomplish his mission. He knew that many others would have been tempted to say they had used the gold to bribe the New Zealanders and keep it for themselves. Abram's starting salary would be double of what he was paid by the army to run the workshops.

Abram went to see Ben-Gurion, who was also Defense Minister, and told him about his intention to leave. Ben-Gurion asked him why, but did not try to influence his decision. Abram also went to say good-bye to Moshe Dayan.

In 1959 Abram started building his house on land he, as well as 200 other World War II officers, had received as a grant. Things were going well for Israel. New immigrants were coming in; new universities were opening. The people of Israel loved and cherished their new country. New businesses were springing up and trade with other countries grew. Then, unexpectedly, dark clouds appeared on the horizon, and with them, a new threat to Israel's existence.

Egypt's President Nasser felt threatened because Syria, which was receiving strong backing and large supplies of modern weapons from the Soviet Union, turned against him. The Syrians were accusing him of cowardice, of hiding from Israel behind the skirts of the United Nations. Jordan, Iraq, Saudi Arabia, and other Arab countries joined Syria in painting Nasser as a coward. In response to the Soviet machinations and Arab insults, Nasser decided to act. He started making speeches to Egyptian and other Arab audiences, and millions of his countrymen were cheering as he delivered his belligerent diatribes against Israel.

On May 15, 1967, Nasser put all Egyptian armed forces on maximum alert. In violation of the United Nations agreement, he sent his troops into the Sinai toward Israel's borders. Israeli leaders did their best to avoid war. The Eshkol government reassured Nasser that Israel had no aggressive intentions toward any Arab country, particularly against Egypt. All this was for naught.

On May 8 the Egyptian government gave notice to U Thant, the Secretary General of the United Nations, to terminate the presence of its Expeditionary Force on the Egypt-Israeli borders. The United Nations, under pressure, announced it would comply. The Sinai Desert, which was considered by Israel as a defensive buffer, suddenly lost its usefulness. Eshkol and his cabinet knew of Nasser's threat to close the Straits of Tiran to Israeli shipping, but failed to warn Nasser decisively against actually doing it. On May 22, Nasser indeed announced the closing of the Gulf of Aqaba to Israeli shipping, and to all ships from other countries carrying strategic materials to Israel. He added, brazenly, "They, the Jews, threaten war (if the Straits are closed); we tell them: Welcome, we are ready for war."

Eshkol's response was very mild, and he was immediately accused by many Israelis of being a coward for not standing up to Nasser. In addition to trying to avoid bloodshed, Eshkol was playing for time. Israel was taken by surprise by the speed of developments, and needed time to mobilize its own forces and prepare for war.

The Arabs were celebrating. It seemed that Israel was too scared to fight them this time. King Hussein came to Cairo and placed his army under Egyptian command. Nasser became victory-drunk without achieving victory as yet. On May 29 he, in effect, denounced the Partition agreement. He wanted all of Palestine — no more Israel. Eshkol continued his pacific, defensive posture. He didn't have Nasser's charisma. He made a speech on May 28 during which he was fumbling and forgetting his lines. The Israeli people were in a dark mood. Soldiers were furious; they were beating on their radios while listening to Eshkol's speech. There were calls for Eshkol to hand over the Ministry of Defense to Dayan. Even the U.S. government, which until then had warned both parties that it would strongly condemn anyone who would start a war, was sending signals that it understood Israel's beleaguered position.

On June 1, Moshe Dayan, in fact, was named Defense Minister, while Eshkol remained Prime Minister. The government was expanded to include the opposition, and Menachem Begin, the former head of the Irgun, became a member of the Cabinet.

Nasser was caught in his own trap. He could clearly see that Israel's attitude was changing, but he was too caught up in his promises to Arabs everywhere to suddenly lift the blockade of the Straits of Tiran. He still didn't believe that Israel would attack first, and was totally surprised when the Israeli Air Force, led by General Weizmann, sent its planes flying low over Mediterranean waters to avoid detection, and attacked important Egyptian military airfields. In one swoop, they destroyed the bulk of the entire Egyptian Air Force. Dayan was smart, and withheld any war communiques announcing this decisive victory. Cairo, on the other hand, started broadcasting stories about fictitious Egyptian victories. Nasser, in order to entice King Hussein to enter the war, told him that 75 percent of the Israeli Air Force was destroyed, and that Egyptian tanks had penetrated deep into Israel. Israelis were sending their own signals to the King telling him that Nasser was lying, and that in fact, Israel achieved a smashing victory. This news could not stop Hussein. Within hours, Jordan and Syria entered the war against Israel, having no inkling that Egypt's armed forces were already crippled.

Now Israel's war planes turned their attention to the east and north, and in short order, destroyed the Syrian as well as the Jordanian Air Force. Brigadier Ariel Sharon was in the forefront of a ground offensive which quickly defeated the Egyptian armies, occupied the Gaza Strip, and advanced at a headlong pace toward the Suez Canal. Once they broke the back of the Egyptian Army, Israel's soldiers drove Hussein's forces back into Jordan, and captured the entire West Bank and the Jordanian held sections of Jerusalem.

Israeli soldiers prayed at the captured West Wall, and it was an emotional moment indeed. Then they attacked the Syrian Army and even succeeded in seizing the Golan Heights. A former Jewish-British officer by the name of Carmel led the as-

sault. Israeli soldiers had to climb steep walls in the face of withering Syrian artillery fire to capture the Heights in a single day.
The taking of the Golan won its place in history books as one of
the bravest and most amazing military feats of all times. It put
to rest forever the anti-Semitic claims that Jews are cowards,
afraid to risk their lives.

The Six Day War itself was one of the most stunning and ex-
plosive military campaigns in history. The combined Arab
armies that the Jews defeated were not at all like the ones they
were fighting in the War of Independence. These were trained
by Russian military experts, and equipped with the latest mod-
els of fighter and bomber airplanes, tanks, artillery etc., supplied by Russia and other countries.

Jewish hearts everywhere were filled with pride and joy.
There were wild celebrations all over Israel. Moshe Dayan became not only a Jewish, but an international hero. His photo,
with a patch over one eye, was featured on the cover of *Time*
magazine, as well as on the covers of magazines all over the
world.

Hy was in the infantry, and his unit wound up, in a few days,
at the Suez Canal. Abram himself was surprised by the ability of
the Israeli Air Force to destroy virtually all Egyptian military
planes with one quick blow.

An interesting vignette in a life of an Israeli soldier:

> The price we pay . . . It was the fifth day of the
> Six Day War. It was 1:30 A.M. Abram was driving from
> Naharia towards Tel Aviv. There was no traffic on
> the road, not a single car. No sign of life; everybody
> was mobilized.
>
> When Abram reached the outskirts of Haifa, he
> saw a lonely soldier standing on the side of the road
> trying to catch a tram. It was hopeless. Abram
> stopped immediately and picked him up. The sol-

dier was extremely nervous. He told Abram he had been trying for hours to get transportation, but to no avail. His unit was in the front line at the Syrian border. He had been released and ordered to go home immediately. He was told something important had happened to his family.

He had a brother in the army fighting somewhere, and a brother-in-law fighting somewhere else, but he had no idea where they were.

When they reached Natania, the soldier asked Abram to let him off. Abram told him that he wouldn't mind taking him home, wherever he lived, but the soldier refused.

He said to Abram, "I want to have another 15 minutes for myself," he added, "I know what news is awaiting me — either my brother is dead, or my brother-in-law is dead, or both of them are." Abram sat for quite a while without saying a word. He knew the soldier was right.

EPILOGUE

The ensuing years were good for Abram. There were a few days of anxiety when the Arab states again ganged up on Israel and launched a sneaky attack on the Holy Day of Yom Kippur in 1973. But after a few days, Israel's Army recovered from the surprise and again defeated the Arabs decisively.

Unexpectedly, the Egyptian President, Anwar Sadat, paid a visit to Israel and negotiated a peace agreement with Menachem Begin, then Prime Minister of Israel. A peace treaty was signed in Washington. One of the key players was President Jimmy Carter who put in a great deal of time and energy to facilitate the agreement.

Abram and his family live now in the house which Abram built with his own hands. He continued his work at the insurance company until a few years ago. At 84 he is still painting and adding ancient stones to his collection. Around his house there are stones of historical value which Abram found in many parts of Israel. A few months ago Abram went to Hrubieszow to design and build a memorial for the Hrubieszow victims of the Holocaust. It's a beautiful wall surrounded on both sides by tombstones from the Jewish cemetery. With the cooperation of the local Polish government, Abram personally spent three weeks in Hrubieszow obtaining materials and building the memorial.

Abram is an unusual man in today's world. A man of total integrity, great courage, great intelligence, and many talents. Israel, which he risked his life so many times for, is still the love of his life.